TYRONE WILLINGHAM

THE MEANING OF VICTORY

Fred Mitchell

TYRONE WILLINGHAM

THE MEANING OF VICTORY

Publisher: **Peter L. Bannon**
Senior Managing Editors: **Susan M. Moyer and Joseph J. Bannon, Jr.**
Coordinating Editor: **Noah Amstadter**
Art Director: **K. Jeffrey Higgerson**
Graphic Designer: **Christine Mohrbacher**
Copy Editor: **Cynthia L. McNew**

Front cover photo:
Andy Kenna/The Observer
Back cover photo:
Michael and Susan Bennett/Lighthouse Imaging

www.SportsPublishingLLC.com
ISBN: 1-58261-672-8

This book and its pages are dedicated to my wife, Kim, and our son, Cameron. They represent my daily inspirations.

TABLE OF CONTENTS

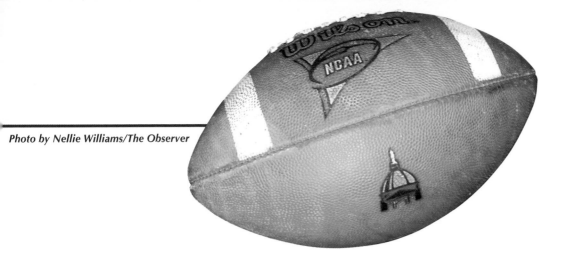

Photo by Nellie Williams/The Observer

INTRODUCTION

Stoic, unflappable, determined—all words used to describe Tyrone Willingham—represent the remarkable character of a man whose entire life has demanded poise under pressure.

While Willingham became a household name during his first season as head football coach of the Fighting Irish of Notre Dame, this book goes behind the scenes and listens to the voices of the people who helped shape the athlete, the coach and the man.

From his roots in Kinston, N.C., to his playing career at Michigan State and his 18-year coaching odyssey that included stops at his alma mater, Stanford and the NFL, we observe how every assignment was for a purpose.

Whether he was performing as an athlete or a coach, Willingham, it seems, was never anybody's first choice. But he always responded in a first-class manner. A walk-on athlete at Michigan State, Willingham earned three letters each in football and baseball.

As perhaps the fourth or fifth choice to become head coach at Notre Dame, Willingham answered the call and led the Irish to a 10-3 record and a bowl appearance in his first season.

Bob Davie had been fired as Notre Dame's head coach after the disappointing 5-6 season of 2001. Willingham then replaced George O'Leary, who had been forced to resign because of embellishments on his resume. Willingham became the first African-American head coach in the history of Notre Dame.

"Life is not perfect," Willingham says. "There are going to be some times in your job that things are not going to be going the way you want them to go, and you can't quit. You can't just storm off."

A disappointing loss to North Carolina State in the Gator Bowl left a bitter taste in the mouth of Willingham, the perfectionist. But Notre Dame fans must realize: This is no time to quit, no time to just storm off.

Willingham says he feels "unworthy" of having a book written about him. "I have so much more to accomplish. The job is not done by any means."

But the true measure of Willingham should not be calculated on the basis of how many football games he wins. Or how many championship teams he oversees. His message has been conveyed by the manner in which he approaches life's challenges, both on the field and off.

"I hope anything that I do in my life will be very positive, because I'd like for my kids to look at their father and say he had a life that was very positive and he fulfilled his dreams and the dreams of others," Willingham told Chicago's Sporting News Radio (WCSN) last fall.

"To me it's very simple: How can I as an athletic director or administrator make my university better? All you have to do is choose the right person. Color has nothing to do with it, just choosing the right person. He could be black, white, green—it's that simple to me. When you do that, you make your organization better. If an athletic director is concerned with revenue, then with the right person, you gain revenue, you gain the right image, and it's just that simple."

This book allows several other people to tell the compelling Tyrone Willingham story—people somehow inspired by his remarkable resolve to do the very best he can in every phase of his life.

Fred Mitchell

Fred Mitchell   August 2003

The Meaning of Victory

CHAPTER 1

KEEPING SCORE

Blacks are grossly underrepresented amongst college football coaches, but Willingham's success could help change the trend

Photo by Brian Pucevich/The Observer

We all need to keep score in the world of sports. It's the American way.

How many touchdowns did he score? How many baskets did he convert? And how much does he make?

So it should come as little surprise that coaching scorecards come under routine scrutiny in both the professional and collegiate ranks.

Of the nation's 117 major college football teams in 2002, only four began the season led by black head coaches, including Notre Dame's Tyrone Willingham. According to *USA Today*, only 12 major college programs—just 10 percent—have even one African-American among their chief assistant coaches.

Has this, too, become the American way?

"The fact that there have been only 20 colleges that have had a black a head coach in the history of college football is nothing short of a disgrace," Richard Lapchick, chairman of Central Florida's sports business management program, wrote in a letter distributed by the Black Coaches Association.

An executive committee was formed in 2002 to analyze the plight of African-American head coaches and head coaching candidates in the NFL. There were just two black coaches in the NFL in 2002—Tony Dungy of the Indianapolis Colts and Herman Edwards of the New York Jets. At the end of the 2002 season, Marvin Lewis was named head coach of the Cincinnati Bengals.

The committee, which includes attorneys Johnnie Cochran and Cyrus Mehri, applied methods of statistical analysis similar to those developed in civil rights enforcement cases at major corporations such as Texaco, Coca-Cola, Johnson & Johnson and BellSouth.

"We believe there is a lesson from Notre Dame to be learned by the teams of the National Football League, which repeatedly overlooked Tyrone Willingham as a potential coach," Mehri and Cochran wrote.

"Wins and losses—the currency of football and all team sports—form the statistical heart of this report. We created a database including the win-loss records of each head coach in the NFL over the last fifteen years. We

When Willingham's Fighting Irish faced Bobby Williams's Michigan State Spartans on Sept. 21, 2002, the game marked the first time Division I-A black head coaches from BCS conferences faced each other. Williams would be fired before season's end. *Photo by AP/WWP*

> *"The fact that there have been only 20 colleges that have had a black head coach in the history of college football is nothing short of a disgrace."*
>
> —Richard Lapchick, **Chairman of Central Florida's Sports Business Management Program**

Attorneys Johnnie Cochran, right, and Cyrus Mehri, second from right, lead a news conference concerning minority hiring in the NFL on Jan. 22, 2003 in San Diego. Former NFL stars Kellen Winslow, left, and Warren Moon also answered questions. Cochran and Mehri are members of the executive committee of the Black Coaches Association. *Photo by AP/WWP*

then asked labor economist Dr. Janice Madden of the University of Pennsylvania to analyze this database and compare the overall performance of the five African-American head coaches [Art Shell, Dennis Green, Dungy, Ray Rhodes and Edwards] with all other head coaches during this period."

Madden determined that:

•The black coaches averaged 1.1 more wins per season than white coaches.

•The black coaches led their teams to the playoffs 67 percent of the time versus 39 percent of the time for the white coaches.

•In their first season, black coaches averaged 2.7 more wins than the white coaches in their first season.

•In their final season, terminated black coaches win an average of 1.3 more games than terminated white coaches.

•The black coaches inherited teams with an average of 7.4 wins per season and, during their tenures, increased the average wins for their teams to 9.1 per season.

The report was submitted to the NFL, and the committee was encouraged by the initial response of league spokesman Greg Aiello in October of 2002.

"Johnnie Cochran and I issued our report—'Black Coaches in the National Football League: Superior Performance, Inferior Opportunities,'" Mehri said. "The report contains a proposal called the 'Fair Competition Resolution' that would require each NFL team to interview a racially diverse final candidate slate for vacant head coaching positions—or opt out by forfeiting a significant draft choice.

"We applaud the NFL for taking the issue seriously and acknowledging that there is significant room for improvement."

According to the proposal, teams could receive extra draft picks for having a racially diverse front office. The resolution also gives the commissioner the right to award supplemental draft choices to teams that have minority candidates in jobs such as general manager.

In a sport where 43 percent of the players are black, college administrators routinely ignore the lack of diversity in the most coveted college football coaching positions. Privately, college executives trot out the tired refrain that trusted alums feel uncomfortable supporting a program led by a minority.

Mehri says: "If, in 2002, we're no better off than 1924, something's wrong."

And all of this time we thought the idea was to win games and do your best to give your athletes an opportunity to graduate.

The BCA committee also wrote: "During the 2002 hiring cycle, NFL fans watched African-American coaching pioneers such as Tony Dungy and Dennis Green terminated despite their winning programs. Meanwhile Marvin Lewis, arguably one of the most dynamic and gifted head coaching candidates, could not obtain a meaningful opportunity to compete for a head coaching position [until the end of 2002]. Despite the success of other professional sports leagues, notably the NBA, in providing greater opportunity for African-American coaching candidates, the owners of the NFL franchises continue to disappoint. To prompt real advancement on this issue, we include with this Report a Fair Competition Resolution, which we call on the commissioner to bring before the team owners for a vote, prior to the next hiring cycle."

The college enrollment of minority students has increased 57 percent nationwide since the 1980s. But those percentages are not reflected in the most visible athletic leadership positions across the country.

John Thompson, the former longtime Georgetown University basketball coach, has a practical perspective on the plight of black assistants seeking head coaching positions.

"Unfortunately, in our society, we still have a lot of people who, because they do not socialize with or go to church with or operate in business with a lot of minorities, they are not comfortable enough to make decisions that relate to minorities progressing in society," said Thompson. "I think the Black Coaches Association sometimes can bridge that gap, or organizations like the BCA, to help create that comfort level.

"In a lot of areas, there has been change, but by the same token, I think there is a need for more," said Thompson. "There is a responsibility on our side, too, to put ourselves in a position where we can take advantage of those opportunities. People don't prepare themselves for things they know they do not have a chance to participate in. It is interesting for [employers] to run around and say they can't find a lot of qualified [minorities]. When I see [a black person] as a writer, I know that there is a possibility of a student that I have becoming a writer. But if I never see you as a writer, then there is no need for me to prepare that student to become a writer."

Thompson always has been outspoken in his views about racial inequality in sports and society. Other successful minority coaches, including Indianapolis Colts boss Tony Dungy, have taken a more subtle approach.

"There is room for more than one way of getting things accomplished. That is my personality," said Dungy, who toiled silently for years as a highly qualified assistant before receiving a chance to become a head coach in the NFL.

"I think people should follow their heart," added Thompson. "We should also realize that we are not just representing ourselves. Unfortunately, in this society, so many people reflect on your ability to do something based on what they see another minority, another black do. And that's just the reality of it. We have to be careful in some instances with that."

A recently released National Collegiate Athletic Association study shows that among athletic directors, who have the primary responsibility for hiring coaches, the number of blacks dropped to less than three percent at major colleges in 2001, down from four percent in 1995.

So what is the solution?

Floyd Keith, executive director of the Black Coaches Association, says his organization and others intend to create a Hiring Report Card by August 2003 to grade the progress of colleges hiring minority football coaches.

"We can't tell [recruits] where to go to school," Keith said. "What we would like is that if a person has five choices, we want them to look and see if there is a program that shows diversity in hiring."

Keith says he is even considering using clothing to get the word out about schools that fail to hire minorities for key positions.

"If you saw someone walking past you with a shirt that said 'Don't Play Where You Can't Coach,' I think that speaks a lot," he said.

Keith says the BCA would re-evaluate its three-year plan and consider other ways to force changes if significant progress is not reached by August 2004.

"Ten years from now, I hope we don't have to have a press conference about hiring issues," Keith said.

"We're not trying to say a student athlete doesn't have a right to go someplace and get a quality education.

National Security Advisor Dr. Condoleezza Rice, who earned her master's degree from Notre Dame in 1975 and served as Stanford University's provost, shares a moment with good friend Tyrone Willingham after Notre Dame's win over Maryland. *Photo by Michael and Susan Bennett/ Lighthouse Imaging*

Former Georgetown coach John Thompson speaks at a Jan. 8, 1999 news conference to announce his retirement from coaching. Thompson, who has always been outspoken in his views about racial inequality in sports and society, says organizations like the Black Coaches Association help bridge the social gap between employees and minorities. *Photo by AP/WWP*

But he should have a right to go and play someplace where diversity is stressed."

Major League Baseball initiated a system three years ago requiring teams with managerial openings to submit a list of final candidates to the commissioner's office to show whether they were complying with new orders to give minorities a chance.

That was "the one thing that's made the difference," said Lapchick, who wrote the "Racial & Gender Report Card."

The NBA has been at the forefront of hiring black coaches over the past two decades, including Indiana Pacers coach Isiah Thomas.

Thomas, a member of the Basketball Hall of Fame, retired in May 1994, and his No. 11 jersey has been retired by the Detroit Pistons.

He then became part owner and general manager of the Toronto Raptors before acquiring the Continental

Basketball Association for $10 million.

Now he is back in the NBA as the Pacers' coach. "I will always put mountains in front of myself to climb," Thomas says.

"In the NBA we don't even notice any more who is hired and fired," said Lapchick. "We'd love the NFL to get in that position."

Willingham and Bobby Williams at Michigan State University became the first Division I-A black head coaches from BCS conferences to face each other on Sept. 21, 2002. It had taken almost 40 years since the Civil Rights Act was passed for such an auspicious occasion.

"At least the next time it happens, we can't say it's the first time," said San Jose State football coach Fitzgerald Hill.

Hill, Willingham and Williams represented three-fourths of Division I-A's black coaching foursome in 2002. The other was New Mexico State University's Tony

Floyd Keith, executive director of the Black Coaches Association, answers questions at a news conference in Indianapolis, Tuesday, Oct. 22, 2002. Keith says his organization and others intend to create a Hiring Report Card by August 2003 to grade the progress of colleges hiring minority football coaches. *Photo by AP/WWP*

The lack of diversity in the area of athletic administration is also appalling. Since the NCAA began tracking race demographics of athletics administrators in 1995, there has been little growth for blacks in decision-making positions.

While a sporting nation applauds the performance of Tyrone Willingham, the spotlight shines even brighter on the administrators across the country who routinely overlook qualified minority candidates.

"None of us can be oblivious to facts. They tell the truth," said BCA executive cirector Floyd Keith in the *NCAA News*. "Sometimes we don't realize it—we all like to think we're part of the solution, but none of us likes to think we're part of the problem.

"Hopefully, those who say they support change recognize they have to do more. If you stay status quo, you're part of the problem."

Since coaches such as Willingham have grabbed the attention of our nation's conscience, now should be the time for others in power to act.

In a recent NCAA survey of Division I-A presidents, 78 percent said they saw the diversity issue in football as a primary concern. The NCAA Football Oversight Committee and the Minority Opportunities and Interests Committee have told the Division I Board of Directors to take action. Grant Teaff, executive director of the American Football Coaches Association (AFCA), said his members constantly ask what more can be done to get more minorities into the profession.

The coaches and administrators are starting to talk the talk. But will they walk the walk?

Fitz Hill was an assistant coach at the University of Arkansas before becoming head coach at San Jose State. He thinks of himself foremost as an educator, then as a black coach.

"I'm a sports sociologist who happens to be a football coach who happens to be black," Hill has been quoted as

Samuel. That short list was trimmed to three when Williams was relieved of his duties at MSU at the end of the season.

Those deplorable numbers from 2002 are trumped by even worse data in decades past. Since 1982, there have been 348 head coaching vacancies in Division I-A football. Black coaches have been selected for 18 (five percent) of those positions, with 14 of the hires coming after 1990. Blacks have been selected for only six of the last 109 vacancies.

Notre Dame running backs coach Buzz Preston, left, and secondary coach Trent Walters, right, brought a combined 56 year's experience as assistant coaches in college and the NFL with them to Notre Dame, but neither had ever served as a head coach.
Photos by Nellie Williams/The Observer

saying. Hill is one of just three Division I-A football coaches who has earned a doctorate. Hill wrote his dissertation on examining barriers to coaching opportunities for blacks.

"I am a head coach now, but my research gives me a right to make comments," he said. "I'm reporting facts from data that I've personally collected. I never point a finger; that's not my style. The point is not to make white coaches feel bad—that's not it at all. When you make people feel bad, they cut you off."

Hill has conducted two surveys, one in 1995 and another in 2000, examining racial perceptions of employment opportunities from majority and minority perspectives.

In general, Hill realized that white respondents generally feel there is equal opportunity and access. But black respondents disagreed.

For instance, most black respondents to the survey felt black coaches are hired not for their football expertise, but to help monitor and relate to black athletes. Most white respondents disagreed.

Hill refers to the different perceptions as "rational discrimination," that turns into a mindset. He thinks that white coaches who recruit black players with questionable academic credentials automatically come to believe that blacks in general are not good coaching prospects.

"In the back of your mind, you bring that with you all the way to when you get ready to hire a person," Hill said. "Then you look at a black candidate and you wonder if he's smart enough to be a coordinator and call plays, or play a leadership role. Is this person going to dress well enough, be eloquent enough with alumni?

"You say you're trying to find the best person for the job, but when you do that you don't have a qualified African-American picture that comes to mind."

Hill says he has been on recruiting trips with white assistant coaches where the recruit assumed the white coach was the head coach and Hill was the recruiting coordinator.

"They don't mean it as discriminatory," he said, "but subconsciously it never registers to them that I'm the head football coach because I'm a black coach coming there to get the recruits. That's the mindset. The fact is, since there are so few of us, there's probably never been a black head football coach from Division I come to that school."

The recurring refrain from white administrators is that significant progress has been made on the minority hiring front.

They frequently point to the fact that the percentage of black assistant coaches actually has risen from 18 to 22 percent since 1995.

"They do believe it because they see an influx of black assistant coaches coming into the pipeline," Hill said. "It used to be that only one black was hired per staff and now it's often two or more. So if you're among those schools or you're out on the road recruiting and you keep running into black recruiters, then you might be inclined to think the problem has subsided.

"But the major problem still rests in the contrast of perspectives when it comes to equal opportunity. You have white coaches who think everything's going to be OK, and then you have black coaches who look at the facts and wonder how anyone could think everything is OK. That's the problem."

According to a *USA Today* story, there are just 12 black Division I-A offensive or defensive coordinators. Those are the positions from which head coaches often are chosen.

"Administrators hire white coaches because the vast majority of [administrators] are white," said one respondent to Hill's survey. "In turn, white coaches hire primarily white staffs because they want to work with people they are familiar with. The black coach is then hired to fill a quota, recruit the black athletes and become their mentor."

Another said, "There seems to be a mentality that two black coaches is enough. There's also the perception among the white assistants that we have it made because of our color. What they don't realize is that we are competing for just those two spots out of the nine assistant coaching positions."

"The best thing we can do is to encourage minorities to join the ranks and prepare themselves for opportunities. I guarantee you that Tyrone Willingham was not hired because he is a minority, and I guarantee you that Tyrone Willingham wouldn't want to be hired just because he is a minority."

—Grant Teaff, Executive Director of the American Football Coaches Association

Dr. Fitzgerald Hill, head football coach at San Jose State, conducted two surveys, one in 1995 and another in 2000, examining racial perceptions of employment opportunities from majority and minority perspectives. ***Photo by AP/WWP***

Tyrone Willingham

Still another noted, "I am perceived as the resident 'expert' on all minority affairs. Black players come to me with social, personal and academic problems. This does not set well with others on the staff."

Many white coaches and administrators feel minority coaches gripe too much.

"But I don't think a person could say based on past hiring numbers that there doesn't need to be some sort of process in place to guarantee equal opportunity," Hill said. "At some point, we're going to have to look at Title VII [federal law] to correct the situation if institutions don't correct it themselves. You just can't continue to say, especially when you're receiving federal dollars, that you're hiring the best person when the pool is not open to everyone."

So what are the immediate solutions?

"There's no simple solution," Teaff said. "If there was, it would have been solved."

A letter-writing campaign was deployed last year by the BCA to provide candidates for Division I-A openings. But all of the openings were filled by whites. Notre Dame even hired a white coach—George O'Leary—before Willingham took over the position. And Willingham's hire did not increase the overall numbers, because he already had been at Stanford.

There has been consideration by NCAA committees to legislate incentives for schools to appoint more black graduate assistants. But legal ramifications have stymied such measures.

The hope is that the success by minority football coaches such as Willingham will stir more positive action.

The lack of minority coaches in college basketball persisted until black coaches began winning.

Chicago Cubs manager Dusty Baker embraces Willingham and Notre Dame Alumni Association executive director Chuck Lennon during the pep rally before Notre Dame's home game against Boston College in October, 2002. Baker and Willingham, who are friends, both enjoyed success that fall—Baker leading the San Francisco Giants to the World Series and Willingham's Irish opening with an 8-0 record. *Photo by Michael and Susan Bennett/Lighthouse Imaging*

"A lot of things changed after Texas Western," the BCA's Keith said, referring to coach Don Haskins's team that beat the University of Kentucky in the 1966 national championship game.

It is an unfortunate circumstance that black coaches tend to be judged and evaluated as a group.

"That's the problem we're dealing with," Hill said. "Success for black coaches shouldn't be judged on Tyrone's success or my success; it should be merit-based individually. However, the hiring process is very subjective."

Teaff said an organization cannot change the mindset of institutions.

"Our association has little effect on institutions hiring head coaches," he said. "We have for some time now provided for athletics directors who call a list of top candidates, and minority coaches are included in that, but in the end, it's an institutional decision.

"The best thing we can do is to encourage minorities to join the ranks and prepare themselves for opportunities. I guarantee you that Tyrone Willingham was not hired because he is a minority, and I guarantee you that Tyrone Willingham wouldn't want to be hired just because he is a minority. He has prepared himself to assume the opportunity. It's a delicate balance between those opportunities being created and individuals being prepared when the opportunity comes along."

The AFCA has 10,000 members competing for jobs at 115 Division I-A schools. Therefore many whites and minorities come away disappointed.

"In our profession," Teaff said, "most individuals—minority or non-minority—come in with a dream to go to the top. Not everybody will get that chance. The whole concept is finding ways to increase the percentage of opportunities for minority coaches. They ought to have a bigger bite of the pie. But that doesn't mean that they have any more desire to coach than the non-minority coaches who come in with the same goals and dreams.

"It comes down to preparation and created opportunities. The good thing is that we have a lot of people who are concerned and who are working, and I think eventually we're going to get there. But it's probably kind of painful now, probably for everybody, to tell you the truth."

Meanwhile, college basketball has made major strides in coaching diversity. The latest NCAA research shows that almost 28 percent of Division I head men's basketball coaches are black and that almost 36 percent of assistants are black.

Basketball is perceived as more dominated by minority players, leading to the diversity in head coaches.

Also, the success of black coaches such as Georgetown University's John Thompson and Nolan Richardson of the University of Arkansas helped pave the way.

But it also should be pointed out that college basketball programs do not generate the kind of revenue that major college football does.

"The big money still is in football, and a lot of people are not willing to give that kind of power to a minority," said Ramapo College athletics director Eugene Marshall, who chairs the NCAA Minority Opportunities and Interests Committee.

"Usually the athletics director was the head football coach. It wasn't until 10 to 15 years ago that presidents started hiring ADs who were managers rather than head football coaches," said San Jose State's Hill. "Basketball is a sport that's really just come on to produce great revenue over the past 30 years, unlike football, which always has been the primary revenue producer and has more tradition in that regard."

"If you follow the money you'll usually find the answers to things," said the BCA's Keith. "People who are successful sometimes become oblivious to color. Last time I looked, money was green."

University of Kansas chancellor Robert Hemenway, who chairs the Division I board of directors, says he hopes money is not the guiding force in minority hiring.

"I think it's a false issue to suggest that money is a commodity that's tied to race," he said. "It's wrong for people doing the hiring to think that a black coach would not have the same view of revenue and its importance to football."

Hemenway said he's not sure why football trails other parts of the university when it comes to racial diversity.

"We have tried and true techniques for developing people so that they can be competitive in those searches," he said. "In my experience, minority candidates do not have any trouble competing if they know they're entering

to talk about improving opportunities for black coaches. A three-year strategy for what Keith calls "measurable improvement" was plotted.

The Oct. 22 report calls for short-term and long-term goals in four areas: knowledge (awareness), accountability, political influence and financial influence. One of the goals is to achieve a 20 percent success rate in hiring black football coaches for Division I vacancies

> # *"You say you're trying to find the best person for the job, but when you do that you don't have a qualified African-American picture that comes to mind."*
> —Dr. Fitzgerald Hill, San Jose State Head Coach

into a level playing field. We need to make sure it's a level playing field."

There are many other theories as to why college basketball has embraced coaching diversity more readily than football.

"C. M. Newton was a change agent, along with John Thompson, John Chaney, Clint Bryant and all the way back to Fred Snowden at Arizona State," Marshall said. "Those guys worked hard to make change happen."

The Aug. 23, 2002 Black Coaches Association Classic pitted the University of Nebraska against Texas Christian University.

Keith used the BCA's classic to organize a summit among representatives from the NCAA, NFL and AFCA

(excluding openings at historically black colleges and universities) that open after the end of this season. The BCA wants that to be accomplished by August 2005.

The report also calls for a "hiring report card" for NCAA schools and advocates that the hiring process be included in Division I certification and Divisions II and III self-studies. The NCAA Minority Opportunities and Interests Committee already has supported the latter.

Additionally, the report calls for a "market brand" on a line of apparel that brings the minority hiring issue to the general public. The slogan "Don't Play Where You Can't Coach" would appear on apparel promoting significant sports figures or players who have broken barriers.

Photo by John Althouse

DETERMINED FROM THE START

*Childhood friend **Marion Wigfall** reflects on the drive and dedication shown in Jacksonville, N.C.'s classrooms and ballfields*

Lionel Tyrone Willingham, who was born on Dec. 30, 1953, in Kinston, N.C., graduated from Jacksonville High School in Jacksonville, N.C.

"We grew up on the same street—Kerr Street. And I am about five years older than Tyrone," said Marion Wigfall, now assistant principal at Jacksonville High School. "When I was in high school, Tyrone was in middle school and I was a quarterback on our high school team. I would get up at about 5 o'clock in the morning to start my workouts. Tyrone and his brother, Jerome, would come out a number of those mornings and work out with me. After I would do all my calisthenics and started my throwing, Tyrone would be my running back. I don't know if it was at that point that he got interested in football. Seems like everyone in our neighborhood was interested in football."

The same determined expression Willingham wears now when the television camera pans the Notre Dame sideline was also evident early in his life.

"He always had a desire to achieve," Wigfall recalled. "He had an attitude whereby he would do whatever he had to do to win. He always had that drive; you could always see that in him. He wanted to perform at his best. Tyrone had the same serious look on his face that he has today. He is for real."

Overcoming the odds throughout his life, Willingham used quickness and guile to compensate for his diminutive stature.

"In high school he was short and he wasn't very big. But he always showed the desire and leadership ability in high school," said Wigfall.

Willingham's mother was a teacher, and the importance of education was indelibly etched. But when he wasn't studying, Willingham was testing his skills athletically.

"We all used to hang out at a community center that was right at the end of the street, almost in front of the house that he lived in," said Wigfall. "We all spent a lot of time there. And there was a thing in our neighborhood where the older guys who played high school football would have this bond with the younger guys who played

Jerome Willingham stands in front of the two-story home where he and older brother Tyrone grew up with their parents, Lilian and Nathaniel, and sisters Joyce and Gail. ***Photo by John Althouse***

> *"He always had that drive; you could always see it in him. He wanted to perform at his best."*
>
> —Marion Wigfall, Willingham's Childhood Friend

in middle school. We wanted to pass things on and help them to be the type of athlete they wanted to be.

"There was always a competitive thing in our city as far as the individual neighborhoods. We wanted to have more guys in the starting lineup at Jacksonville High from our neighborhood. And Tyrone always has been a very competitive person."

Wigfall would go on from Jacksonville High School to attend Johnson C. Smith College in Charlotte, N.C. He went into the military before finishing up at Fayetteville State.

He earned his degree in physical education with a minor in health education from Michigan State. He and his wife, Kim, have three children: Cassidy (born 1/10/84), Kelsey (5/9/88) and Nathaniel (7/9/90).

Willingham was an assistant coach on the collegiate and professional levels for 18 years prior to his appointment as Stanford's head coach. During his career as an assistant, he coached on offense, defense and special teams.

A 1977 graduate of Michigan State, Willingham coached under Dennis Green for six seasons—three at

As part of a recent revitalization program, the Jacksonville community named "L.P. Willingham Parkway" in honor of Tyrone's late mother. The street, adjacent to the river, features a median with benches, grass, and flower beds. *Photo by John Althouse*

Willingham later would walk on at Michigan State and play both football and baseball. Willingham went on to earn three letters in each sport. As a quarterback and flanker in football, he was named the team's most inspirational player in 1976. In 1977, Willingham was awarded the Big Ten Conference Medal of Honor as the outstanding scholar athlete in the league. In baseball, he received the sportsmanship award in 1975 and was an All-Big Ten selection in '77.

Stanford and three with the Minnesota Vikings. The Vikings finished 8-8 in 1991, the year before Willingham arrived with Green in Minnesota. In his three seasons in Minnesota, Willingham helped the Vikings win two National Football Conference Central Division championships and advance to the playoffs all three seasons.

In 1992, the Vikings finished 11-5 and won the NFC Central Division championship. Willingham worked with

L.P. Willingham Waterfront Park in Jacksonville is named in honor of Tyrone's late mother, Lilian Willingham. Mrs. Willingham earned a master's degree from Columbia University in New York and taught elementary school in Jacksonville for 38 years. *Photo by John Althouse*

Terry Allen that season. He set a club record by rushing for 1,201 yards. In 1993, Minnesota finished 9-7 and earned a wild card playoff berth. The Vikings won the division title again in '94 and earned another playoff berth with a 10-6 record.

While at Stanford (1989-91), Willingham was part of Green's staff that helped rejuvenate the program. The Cardinal went from 3-8 in '89 to 8-4 in 1991. The '91 season ended with a berth in the Aloha Bowl, Stanford's first postseason appearance in five seasons.

The '91 squad won its final seven regular-season games to finish 8-3 overall, 6-2 in the Pac-10. It was Stanford's best season in five years and first bowl appearance since the 1986 Gator Bowl.

Willingham coached two of the top running backs in Stanford football history during his brief tenure as a Cardinal assistant: Glyn Milburn and Tommy Vardell. Vardell was a first-round NFL pick following the '91 season. Milburn is the fifth leading all-time rusher in Stanford history with 2,178 yards, and he is second in the Cardinal record book in all-purpose running with a three-year total of 5,857 yards. Vardell is sixth all-time at Stanford in rushing with 1,789 yards and first in touchdowns with 37.

In '91, Vardell set a Stanford single-season record for rushing (1,084 yards) and TDs (20) while being named the Academic All-American of the Year. Milburn, who set a Stanford record for all-purpose running in 1990 with Willingham as his coach (2,222 yards), went on to earn first-team All-America honors as an all-purpose player in 1992.

Jerome Willingham, Tyrone's younger brother, is a lawyer and city councilman in Jacksonville. Jerome Willingham keeps his law office across the street from his childhood home on Kerr Street. **Photo by John Althouse**

"Because Tyrone is from Jacksonville N.C....a lot of the students here have become Notre Dame fans."

—Marion Wigfall, Assistant Principal at Jacksonville High

Marion "Buddy" Wigfall, now an assistant principal at Jacksonville High, points to a photo of he and Tyrone Willingham together that he hopes the Notre Dame coach will autograph for him. **Photo by John Althouse**

After graduating from Michigan State in 1977, Willingham continued with the Spartan program as a graduate assistant under head coach Darryl Rogers. In '78-79, Willingham was the defensive secondary coach at Central Michigan University (current Notre Dame director of athletics Kevin White was a member of the Chippewa track coaching staff at that time), with those teams finishing 9-2 and 10-0-1, respectively.

From 1980-82, Willingham was the defensive secondary and special teams coach at Michigan State under head coach Muddy Waters. He moved to North Carolina State University for three seasons (1983-85), where he again coached special teams and the defensive secondary under head coach Tom Reed.

Prior to accepting the position as running backs coach at Stanford under Green, Willingham coached receivers and special teams at Rice University from 1986-88.

To this day, Willingham's legacy at Jacksonville High School continues to be enhanced because of his success at Notre Dame.

"I watch more Notre Dame games and read about them in the paper and on the internet now that Tyrone is the head coach," said Wigfall. "Tyrone came to our high school at the beginning of 2003, and our kids were very much excited. Because Tyrone is from Jacksonville, N.C., and he is the coach at Notre Dame, a lot of the students here now have become Notre Dame fans."

CHAPTER 3
A LEADER EMERGES

*Former Michigan State baseball coach **Danny Litwhiler** remembers a walk-on who became a three-time letter winner in both baseball and football*

Photo Courtesy of Michigan State Sports Information

As an aspiring varsity football and baseball player at Michigan State, Tyrone Willingham came prepared to prove himself time and time again.

"He was a walk-on in baseball and he was a walk-on in football, too," said Danny Litwhiler, the former Michigan State baseball coach who saw firsthand the determination Willingham possesses. "He believed in himself and he still does. He does a great job."

Willingham played the outfield for the Spartans in the mid-1970s and began displaying his leadership qualities at that time.

"His outstanding qualities then were his determination, confidence and his ability to kind of be a stabilizer on the team," said Litwhiler. "The whole ball club respected him. He hustled and never let down with his fielding. He made diving catches, and on the bases he would take off and steal."

Willingham has never forgotten the impact Litwhiler had on his coaching career.

"Ty is the kind of person who remembers people," said Litwhiler. "He has kept in contact with me ever since he graduated. When he was an assistant coach, he contacted me. When he got the head coaching job at Stanford, he contacted me and thanked me for giving him the courage and the ability to lead. Then when he got the job at Notre Dame, he called me up. He has just been a wonderful person."

Litwhiler was honored with the Alumnus of the Year Award during the annual MSU baseball banquet May 19, 2003, at the Michigan Athletic Club and Banquet Center. Several other Spartan greats were in attendance at the event, including Hall of Fame pitcher Robin Roberts and 1974 National League MVP Steve Garvey.

Litwhiler and Roberts were the first players in Michigan State baseball history to have their numbers retired. A ceremony honoring the two Spartan greats took place in MSU's last regular-season game against Penn

Tyrone Willingham

Willingham played four seasons of football at Michigan State from 1973 through 1976 under head coaches Denny Stolz and Darryl Rogers. *Photo Courtesy of Michigan State Sports Information*

After an injury sidelined star quarterback Charlie Baggett in 1973, redshirt freshman Willingham took over behind center and led Michigan State to victories over Purdue, Wisconsin, Indiana and Iowa. *Photo Courtesy of Michigan State Sports Information*

State at Kobs Field. Roberts was named the MSU baseball Alumnus of the Year in 2002.

In 19 seasons (1964-82) as head coach of the Spartans, Litwhiler compiled a 488-362-8 record and coached his 1971 and 1979 teams to the Big Ten championship. He also led his teams to NCAA Tournament appearances in 1978 and 1979 en route to becoming MSU's all-time winningest coach.

"I retired from Michigan State in 1982, and I went with the Cincinnati Reds as a hitting instructor and consultant for the minor leagues until 1988," he said.

Perhaps Willingham inherited his penchant for strict team rules and proper decorum from Litwhiler.

"We always had to wear jackets on the road when we stayed at a hotel," said Litwhiler. "They had to wear a coat and tie. It was an order I had and they lived by it."

Thirteen of Litwhiler's players advanced to the major leagues, including Kirk Gibson, Rick Miller and Garvey. A member of the American Coaches Association College Baseball Coaches Hall of Fame and a recipient of the "Lefty Gomez Award" for outstanding contributions to college baseball, Litwhiler amassed a nine-year record of 189-91 at Florida State before coming to MSU.

"When I was coaching at Michigan State, I had the same policy that I had when I coached at Florida State. I give everybody a chance who wants to come out," he said. "I have a tryout session with 100 ballplayers. They would come out and we would screen them and whittle the roster down to about 40 ballplayers. Everybody had a good shot. Tyrone was a good guy on the Michigan State ball club."

A two-sport star at Michigan State, Willingham played alongside some of the university's greatest athletes. In baseball, Willingham and Al Weston (left) served as co-captains in 1977, when Willingham was named second-team All-Big Ten. On the gridiron, Willingham backed up Charlie Baggett at quarterback. Baggett graduated as the school's all-time leader in total offense. ***Photos Courtesy of Michigan State Sports Information***

Litwhiler takes pride in the number of prominent players who went on to play in the major leagues. But he also has a special place in his heart for Willingham and other walk-ons who carved a niche in MSU baseball lore.

"I remember a guy named Bill Wooley who came out for the team," said Litwhiler. "There were 100 guys trying out before we started whittling them down. He makes it to the final cut and then I cut him. He comes up to me and says: 'Coach, I would like to keep coming out. I think

handling 317 chances in the outfield. He was inducted into the MSU Athletics Hall of Fame in 1994.

"Playing with the Cardinals was a wonderful memory," said Litwhiler. "We won the world championship in 1944 playing against the Browns. And, of course, playing with Stan Musial was just fantastic. He was one of the best hitters I ever saw. I wasn't with Ted Williams, so I didn't see him that much. But I know he was a great hitter, too."

> "*Tyrone didn't go anywhere in baseball [as far as the major leagues], but he did go somewhere as a coach.*"
> —Danny Litwhiler, Willingham's Baseball Coach at Michigan State

I can develop and help you. I will do anything on the ball club. I will do anything to help.'

"I said: 'I'll tell you what. You come out and you be the manager. When you come out, you can take infield practice and practice along with us. But your title will be the manager.' Well, he developed into a first-string shortstop."

Litwhiler played 12 major-league seasons with the Phillies, Cardinals, Braves and Reds and in 1942 became the first professional player to record an errorless season,

Watching Willingham excel in the coaching arena has fascinated Litwhiler.

"Tyrone didn't go anywhere in baseball [as far as the major leagues], but he did go somewhere as a coach," said Litwhiler, who remains in contact with many of his former players.

"I had heart bypass surgery and I was in intensive care for six weeks. I got phone calls and letters from former ballplayers," he said.

Former major leaguer Danny Litwhiler, Willingham's baseball coach at Michigan State, won 488 games in 19 years as the Spartans' head coach. ***Photo Courtesy of Michigan State Sports Information***

After graduating with a degree in physical education in the spring of 1977, Willingham stayed in East Lansing as a graduate assistant that fall. ***Photo Courtesy of Michigan State Sports Information***

Willingham's good rapport with the players and ability to instill discipline served him well as a graduate assistant for the Spartans during the 1977 season. *Photo Courtesy of Michigan State Sports Information*

Tyrone Willingham

> *"His outstanding qualities then were his determination, confidence and his ability to kind of be a stabilizer on the team."*
> —Danny Litwhiler, Willingham's College Baseball Coach

After two seasons as the secondary coach at Central Michigan, Willingham returned to his alma mater in 1980 to coach the Spartans' secondary and special teams under new Michigan State head coach Muddy Waters. *Photo Courtesy of Michigan State Sports Information*

MAKING THE MOST OF AN OPPORTUNITY

Bill Walsh *recalls how Willingham embraced Walsh's Minority Fellowship Program and eventually succeeded the NFL legend as Stanford's head coach*

Photo by David Gonzales/Gonzalesphoto.com

The recurring snapshot associated with Bill Walsh is that of a Pro Football Hall of Fame coach with the San Francisco 49ers. But Walsh's ever-evolving legacy also will be his pioneering effort to diversify the NFL coaching roster. His Minority Coaching Fellowship program helped Tyrone Willingham cut his teeth in the profession at the highest level.

In 1987, Walsh created the Minority Coaching Fellowship program that has produced, among others, Willingham, Cincinnati Bengals head coach Marvin Lewis, and NFL assistants Bobby Turner, Don Martin and Don Treadwell. The NFL later adopted this Fellowship as a league-wide program.

"Initially, people were asked to write a letter of interest and, in a sense, an application. It was a statement about their plans and aspirations. Like an essay," Walsh recalled.

"We interviewed them and we talked to the coaches. So we were pretty selective. Tyrone was one of the very first men who interviewed with us, and he made a great impression on everybody because he was all business. He would take on any task. He was thorough and he did everything with a lot of enthusiasm. He appeared to have much more maturity than the other interns. He had a definite maturity that was beyond his years. And he had a purpose. He was there to learn football and study under us. He was there to take full advantage of this opportunity. He took it very, very seriously. During that process he coached players, he helped us in preseason games and he took an active role. He was a coach, and we were all colleagues. So we all worked very closely.

"We also had Marvin Lewis, Bobby Turner, and a number of other guys who were either in that class or a subsequent one. But Tyrone did very well. We knew he had the potential to become a successful head coach. But I wasn't thinking of the NFL. I was thinking of college football. I felt he was ideally suited for college football."

Under Walsh's direction, the 49ers won three Super Bowl titles (1981, '84 and '88), made seven NFC postseason appearances, and claimed six NFC West

> *"Tyrone was one of the very first men who interviewed with us, and he made a great impression on everybody because he was all business."*
> —Bill Walsh, Creator of the Minority Coaching Fellowship

Willingham and former Stanford and San Francisco 49ers coach Bill Walsh greet one another before the October 3, 1998 Notre Dame-Stanford game at Notre Dame. *Photo by David Gonzales/Gonzalesphoto.com*

Tyrone Willingham

division championships. He was twice named NFL Coach of the Year (1981, 1984) and was later named NFL Coach of the Decade for the 1980s.

Walsh became one of only 14 coaches in the history of professional football to be elected to the Hall of Fame when he was enshrined in 1993. He compiled a .617 winning percentage with a 102-63-1 career record that included 10 wins in 14 postseason games. He was the first coach in team history to reach the 100-win plateau.

Walsh took over a losing 49ers team in 1979 and turned it into the most successful NFL franchise over the last two decades. He stepped down as vice president/general manager on May 2, 2001 and is now a consultant.

Walsh had returned to the 49ers as GM on Jan. 20, 1999, with the idea of rectifying San Francisco's salary cap problems. He added younger players, including five rookie starters on defense, and significantly trimmed the payroll.

He originally was appointed the team's general manager in 1982 and ascended to the role of president in 1985. During this period, Walsh was responsible for all major organizational decisions. During the 10-year tenure (1979-88), Walsh directed a perennially contending franchise. Beginning in 1983, the 49ers enjoyed an unprecedented streak of 16 consecutive 10-win seasons. In 1979, he took over a team that went 2-14 the previous season and transformed it into a Super Bowl champion in just three seasons.

Walsh's first collegiate head coaching job came at Stanford in 1977, where he directed the Cardinal to a 17-7 record and captured wins in the Bluebonnet and Sun Bowls during his two-year tenure. Walsh returned to Stanford in 1992 and immediately led the Cardinal to a 10-3 record that concluded with a New Year's Day win over Penn State in the Blockbuster Bowl. It was the school's first New Year's Day bowl game victory in 21 years. He remained at Stanford through the 1994 season.

Willingham and fellow assistant coach Brian Billick encourage the Cardinal players during Stanford's 38-21 win over Cal in 1991. Billick went on to win a Super Bowl as coach of the Baltimore Ravens. **Photo by David Gonzales/Gonzalesphoto.com**

Willingham won 44 games, lost 36 and tied one during his seven seasons as Stanford's head coach.
Photo by David Gonzales/Gonzalesphoto.com

Stanford running backs coach from 1989-91 under Green, Willingham returned to Stanford as head coach Nov. 28, 1994, replacing Walsh. In seven years in Palo Alto, Willingham took the Cardinal to four bowl games, the 1999 Pacific-10 Conference championship and the school's first Rose Bowl appearance in 28 years. Willingham twice was honored by his peers as the Pac-10 Coach of the Year (1995 and 1999) and ranks as the only Stanford coach to earn that honor more than once.

"Coaching at a school such as Notre Dame—and maybe 30 other programs in the country—the coach has so many obligations, so many commitments and expectations," said Walsh. "Not only in coaching, but throughout the year to deal with fundraisers and community gatherings. You just have to be a man for all seasons. It is much more demanding from that aspect than coaching in the NFL. In the NFL when the season is over, you go back to your facility and work on the draft. It's an intense environment, but there are not high expectations to make appearances every day and go through the recruiting process. So the college coach at Notre Dame and some of the other powerful football schools—it's tougher than in the NFL.

"There's an ongoing series of actions that you have to deal with constantly on the major college level: academics, faculty relations, community relations, media relations. Particularly for a school like Notre Dame, there are overwhelming duties. Tyrone is so well organized and so concise in everything he does. He handles that situation beautifully."

In 1994, Walsh was instrumental in the establishment and management of the World League of American Football, now known as NFL Europe. He has continued to serve the league as a consultant and representative in various NFL ventures.

"There are a lot of coaches, minority or non-minority, who never do get a chance," said Walsh. "They end up on the high school level and do very well and have a great life. Or they coach at a smaller college or get jobs that have no future whatsoever and fail. Sometimes, no matter how good the coach is, you are not going to attract the athletes that you need. You have to think that there are many minority coaches who never have near this option. So the Minority Fellowship program has been very successful. Tyrone is a unique man. Somehow or another, my guess is that he would have succeeded on his own. He would have been fine and done very well."

Walsh also has had a major impact on the coaching careers of several former assistants, including Dennis Green, Mike Holmgren, Mike Shanahan, Ray Rhodes, Jeff Fisher, Sam Wyche, Rod Dowhower, Bruce Coslet, Sherman Lewis, Brian Billick, Gary Kubiak, George

Willingham leads his Stanford team onto the field before the 2000 Rose Bowl. Wisconsin defeated Stanford, 17-9.
Photo by David Gonzales/Gonzalesphoto.com

Seifert, Jon Gruden, Paul Hackett, Tom Holmoe, Dwaine Board, Bobb McKittrick, Bill McPherson, Tom Rathman, Harry Sydney and Tom Lovat.

"Dennis Green really networked with Tyrone, and when Denny went to Stanford, Tyrone followed him right away. And the rest is history," said Walsh. "The networking

After 10 seasons with San Francisco, Walsh joined NBC Sports in 1989 and teamed with renowned announcer Dick Enberg for three seasons as the network's top analyst on NFL and Notre Dame telecasts.

Walsh, who is author of two books—*Finding the Winning Edge* and *Building a Champion*—marveled at the

Willingham motivates his Stanford players in the locker room during their 50-22 win at Arizona in 1999.
Photo by David Gonzales/Gonzalesphoto.com

that we did with him really has made a difference in his career. He got the opportunities that he may not have gotten otherwise. He jumped two or three levels to come to Stanford, then to Minnesota and then back to Stanford as the head coach. If he had remained at Rice, who is to say how he would have done. He would have done very well, but it may have been going through small colleges or things of that level without ever achieving what he has at this level of competition."

way Willingham guided the Fighting Irish to a 10-3 record in his first season at the helm at Notre Dame.

"It's the biggest job in all of coaching, and it is one of the toughest," said Walsh. "Notre Dame will inherently attract athletes who can win seven games. A coach can exist on that level for a while. And then they will find another coach. So the difference at Notre Dame is going from seven wins to 10 wins. And that really takes an excellent coach and an excellent recruiter and a fine

Willingham shares a moment on the sideline with Stanford alumnus Tiger Woods prior to Stanford's win over Texas in 2000.
Photo by David Gonzales/Gonzalesphoto.com

> *"Before Tyrone, that team was destined to win five or six games. And Tyrone took them that far. It was a very significant coaching job."*
>
> —Former Stanford and San Francisco 49ers Coach Bill Walsh on Willingham's First Season at Notre Dame

coaching staff. That's because seven of the 11 games are against really tough competition. Now, they always have a Navy and some other schools on the schedule. Those are the automatics. When it comes to the big games like Michigan, they are going to have comparable if not better talent. My estimate would be that if they played the Florida schools [each year], Notre Dame would be out-manned. If they were to play Michigan and Michigan State, they certainly would not have any advantage. Notre Dame would be out-manned. Notre Dame can do very well, but in order to get over the top, it takes a great coach."

In addition to compiling a 10-2 regular-season record and earning a berth in the Toyota Gator Bowl, Willingham became the first coach in the history of Notre Dame football to win 10 games in his first season. He also guided the Irish to the third best turnaround in school history (plus-4.5 games).

But the resounding loss to USC helped remind Willingham and his troops just how far they have to go to become a national champion.

"Tyrone was revealed to the public, so to speak, when his team was beaten very badly by USC," said Walsh. "That demonstrated that Tyrone had done an incredible job to get his team that far. Because his team was simply not that good. He just took that team and pulled it along with him. They won all of those close games, amazingly, because of Tyrone Willingham. It just wasn't a Notre Dame team that was so talented that it would win 10 games. Tyrone had to just shove the team through that to develop that football team. It was one of the best teams in the country. Then they were, in a sense, undressed by a great team. It became very obvious what Tyrone had done. He had just done a brilliant coaching job. Before Tyrone, that team was destined to win five or six games. And Tyrone took them that far. It was a very significant coaching job."

Willingham poses with the Legends Trophy after Stanford's 17-13 win over Notre Dame in Palo Alto on Nov. 24, 2001. Within 40 days, Willingham would leave Stanford for Notre Dame. *Photo by David Gonzales/Gonzalesphoto.com*

CHAPTER 5

A FAVORABLE IMPRESSION

Dennis Green *explains how working with Willingham in 1986 led Green to bring the young assistant along to Stanford and the Minnesota Vikings*

Photo by David Gonzales/Gonzalesphoto.com

One of the most significant early influences on Tyrone Willingham was former college and NFL head coach Dennis Green.

"I coached in the Big Ten as an assistant from 1974-76. So I remember Tyrone when he played in the Big Ten," said Green. "I had a lot of respect for Tyrone, because you read media guides about guys and I saw that he was initially a walk-on, playing baseball and football. He walked on for both sports, so I was really impressed with him. He was very competitive, playing quarterback and wide receiver. Basically, he could do whatever Michigan State needed him to do."

Green would go on to distinguish himself by owning the most successful record in the National Football League during the 1990s. He has the ninth best winning record in NFL history and held the best winning percentage of NFL active coaches. Green has the highest winning percentage in the Minnesota Vikings' 40-year history. And the 15-1 1998 season was the second best in NFL history.

Other highlights from Green's illustrious coaching career include:

•Most trips to the playoffs, 1992-2000, with seven different quarterbacks.

•The only coach to reach the playoffs in each of the five seasons of 1996-2000.

•Coach of the only team to qualify for the playoffs each of the four years of 1997-2000

•His three-year stretch of 1998-2000 were the best three seasons in a row in Vikings history.

•One of only three to coach a team to win 15 games in a single season.

•One of only eight men in NFL history to lead his team to the playoffs in each of his first three seasons (1992-1994) as a head coach.

But the ties between Willingham and Green began much earlier. Green, who now lives in San Diego with his wife Marie and children, is concentrating on sports marketing and creative consulting projects. He had been a standout halfback with the University of Iowa. As a

Assistant coach Tyrone Willingham listens attentively to then Stanford head coach Dennis Green during Stanford's 38-21 victory over Cal in the 1991 Big Game. *Photo by David Gonzales/Gonzalesphoto.com*

> ## "I think Tyrone showed me early on that he really understood the game of football."
>
> —Dennis Green, Former Stanford and Minnesota Vikings Head Coach

Head coach Dennis Green (far right) and assistant Tyrone Willingham lead the Stanford players onto the field in 1991. Willingham served under Green as running backs coach from 1989 through 1991. *Photo by David Gonzales/Gonzalesphoto.com*

Tyrone Willingham

coach he later helped revive losing programs at Northwestern and Stanford.

"I knew Sherman Lewis pretty well, and he coached Tyrone at Michigan State [as an assistant]," recalled Green. "When Tyrone graduated, Sherman was influential in getting Tyrone to go into the coaching business. The first time Tyrone and I had ever worked together was 1986. He came to work with the San Francisco 49ers with Marvin Lewis. They were on the minority coaching program that Bill Walsh had started. It is a very well-known program now. But Bill Walsh was the first guy to start it. He came up with the concept and the idea. Getting Ty Willingham and Marvin Lewis [now head coach of the Cincinnati Bengals] really assured that the program was going to be successful. Those were two of the best guys you could have. Sherman Lewis was on our staff at the time, and when Tyrone interviewed with me and everyone else, we were all very impressed with him. I was lucky because I was working with the receivers at the time on the offense, and Tyrone helped me. I knew at that time that if I ever had the opportunity to be a head coach again, Tyrone would be one of the first guys that I would call. And I hoped that he would be available to come work with me. That happened when I went to Stanford in 1989."

With the Stanford Cardinal, Willingham continued to exhibit traits that would earn untempered respect from his colleagues and players.

"I think Tyrone showed me early on that he really understood the game of football," said Green. "Also, he loved the competitive aspect of it. He loved the idea of people going out and doing the best that they could do. He was a hard-working guy. And he understood loyalty in the business. He really knew his craft. He could coach quarterbacks, he could coach receivers, he could coach running backs and he could coach defensive backs. So he was very versatile. And he has coached a lot of those positions throughout his coaching career."

After serving as Stanford running backs coach from 1989-91 under Green, Willingham returned to Stanford as head coach Nov. 28, 1994, replacing legendary

Minnesota Vikings running backs coach
Tyrone Willingham surveys the field during
a 1994 practice. Willingham left the Vikings
after the season to take the head coaching
position at Stanford University.
Photo © Rick A. Kolodziej

Willingham followed Dennis Green from Stanford to the NFL's Minnesota Vikings before the 1992 season. Willingham spent three seasons as the Vikings' running backs coach. **Photo © Rick A. Kolodziej**

professional and college coach Bill Walsh. In seven years at Stanford, Willingham took the Cardinal to four bowl games, the 1999 Pac-10 Conference championship and the school's first Rose Bowl appearance in 28 years.

Willingham twice was honored as the Pac-10 Coach of the Year (1995 and 1999)—and ranks as the only Stanford coach to earn that honor more than once.

His 2001 Stanford team enjoyed the best record of his seven seasons, with a 9-3 overall mark, a berth in the Seattle Bowl and final regular-season rankings of ninth in the Bowl Championship Series poll and 11th in both the Associated Press and ESPN/*USA Today* polls.

The 2001 Cardinal went 6-2 in Pac-10 competition for a three-way tie for second place. It marked only the second time in 50 years a Stanford team won nine regular-season games. Three Cardinal players won first-team All-America honors for the first time since 1973. Stanford led the Pac-10 in '01 in scoring (37.1 per game), total

offense (451.5 yards per game), rushing offense (201 yards per game) and rushing defense (109.6 yards per game). The Cardinal finished 17-7 in Pac-10 action from '99 through '01.

In the 2001 NCAA Graduation Rate Report issued last fall, Stanford recorded an 83 percent football graduation rate—fourth in the nation among Division I institutions. The ranking is based on football student athletes who enrolled between 1991 and 1994 (allowing six years for graduation).

In other recent NCAA reports involving football, Stanford ranked second in 2000 (83 percent) and fourth in '99 (81). Stanford and Notre Dame historically rank among the national leaders annually in all the major categories, including all student athletes, football players, plus male, female and African-American student athletes.

"Tyrone really knew what it took to be successful at Stanford. So when he had a chance to go back to Stanford

as a head coach, he was able to be a very successful head coach," said Green. "He was clear about what he was going to bring to it. And I think that is what Notre Dame got from him. He was a guy who didn't need to find out what he was going to do to be successful. They hired a young man who knew exactly what it was going to take to recruit the right kind of players. You can't go in and recruit players to win. You have to win first in order to recruit players. I think he won those guys over because he knew exactly what he wanted to do."

Willingham's strong commitment to maintaining a balance between academic and athletic excellence was recognized by Notre Dame athletic director Kevin White when he was hired to lead the Fighting Irish.

"For the last seven years, Tyrone led the program with the highest academic profile in all of major college football, and over that time he won two conference Coach of the Year awards and took his teams to four bowl games,"

Coach Willingham inspires his players prior to the 2000 season opener against Washington State in Pullman. Stanford won, 24-10. **Photo by David Gonzales/Gonzalesphoto.com**

Coach Willingham speaks to a group of young Stanford fans at the 2000 Spring Game Kids Clinic. **Photo by David Gonzales/ Gonzalesphoto.com**

Tyrone Willingham

> "*[Notre Dame] hired a young man who knew exactly what it was going to take to recruit the right kind of players.*"
> —Dennis Green, Former Stanford Head Coach

Willingham takes a knee to make his point known during Stanford's 2001 Big Game against Cal. The Cardinal won, 35-28, in front of a season-high 71,150 fans. **Photo by David Gonzales/Gonzalesphoto.com**

said White when Willingham was introduced on Jan. 1, 2002, as the new Irish coach.

"I spoke to a great many people about Tyrone—and every one of them regards him as one of the very top coaches in the game today—at the college or pro levels. They regard the job he did at Stanford as simply amazing.

"To the people at the NCAA, he's a man of impeccable integrity; to the recruiting gurus, he's among the very best at attracting talent even when maintaining the highest SAT scores in the nation. He's a disciplinarian whose players love him. He left one of the great universities and one of the great athletic programs in this country to be part of Notre Dame."

Green notes that Willingham's coaching portfolio continues to be stocked with impressive accomplishments that cannot be ignored.

"I think that if Tyrone ever decides to leave Notre Dame—which would be tough to do because Notre Dame is one of the finest universities in the world—I think he will have opportunities in the NFL. When he was an assistant in the NFL he coached Roger Craig with the 49ers and Darren Nelson with the Minnesota Vikings. And he helped us with Robert Smith when we drafted him. Those were all very good football players."

Because of his humble yet tireless approach to coaching, Willingham prefers to have others grade his accomplishments. Dennis Green gives his former pupil high marks.

Playbook in hand, Coach Willingham goes over strategy during Stanford's 21-16 win over USC at the Los Angeles Coliseum on Sept. 29, 2001. *Photo by David Gonzales/Gonzalesphoto.com*

Tyrone Willingham

After taking over at Notre Dame, Willingham continued to display one proud memento of his days at Stanford—his 2000 Rose Bowl ring.
Photo by Michael and Susan Bennett/Lighthouse Imaging

CHAPTER 6

REACHING THE PINNACLE

*Notre Dame's **Kevin White** lauds Coach Willingham for the dignity he brought to a program in turmoil and the team's surprising early success*

Notre Dame athletic director Kevin White was able to rectify the embarrassing hiring of former Georgia Tech football coach George O'Leary at the end of the 2001 season by turning immediately to Tyrone Willingham to lead the Fighting Irish.

O'Leary admitted to a misrepresentation on his résumé, which stated that he had earned a master's degree when in fact he had not. Willingham had been a candidate for the position prior to the O'Leary hiring. When O'Leary was forced to resign immediately, Willingham re-entered the employment picture.

"Due to a selfish and thoughtless act many years ago, I have personally embarrassed Notre Dame, its alumni and fans," O'Leary said in a statement to the university. "The integrity and credibility of Notre Dame is impeccable, and with that in mind, I will resign my position as head football coach effective December 13, 2001."

White responded by saying, "I have accepted the resignation of George O'Leary as head football coach at the University of Notre Dame. George has acknowledged inaccuracies in his biographical materials, including his academic background. I understand that these inaccuracies represent a very human failing; nonetheless, they constitute a breach of trust that makes it impossible for us to go forward with our relationship. I intend to restart our search for a new head football coach immediately."

White knew it was time to turn to Willingham. A press conference to announce the hiring of Willingham was held Jan. 1, 2002. It was indeed a happy New Year for Notre Dame football fans.

"We have spoken to a great many people about this man—people including the commissioner of the Southeastern Conference, Roy Kramer, the general manager of the Chicago Bears, Jerry Angelo, the general manager of the Cleveland Browns, Carmen Policy, Baltimore Ravens head coach Brian Billick, and former Stanford and San Francisco 49ers head coach Bill Walsh," White said during the press conference. "Every one of

A smiling Tyrone Willingham takes a question from the media during the New Year's Day, 2002 press conference to announce his hiring as Notre Dame's 27th head coach.
Photo by Michael and Susan Bennett/Lighthouse Imaging

them regards Tyrone as one of the very top coaches in the game today at the college or pro level. And they regard the job he has done at Stanford as simply amazing.

"I couldn't help but notice that his record beginning this season at Stanford was virtually identical to another record another coach brought here from an academic institution [Northwestern University] some 38 years ago. That coach's name was Ara Parseghian."

Willingham's humble demeanor and subtle humor were demonstrated during his first Notre Dame press conference.

"I am a young man that grew up with parents that loved raising people the right way. They believed that a church was important," he said. "Such mornings we started with Sunday school, followed by church, and of course, if you understand anything about the time schedule of a Methodist church you know that sometimes it can go past 12 noon. And when you understand that and you go back into the day that I was a youngster, you understand that Notre Dame highlights and college football highlights started somewhere around 12 noon.

"So it was part of my responsibility to myself to slip out of church and watch those highlights. So those things, somewhere, were laced in the back of my mind, and I think have brought me to an understanding that this

George O'Leary was originally hired to replace Bob Davie as Notre Dame's head coach following the 2001 season, but was forced to resign after inaccuracies were found on his résumé.
Photo by Nellie Williams/The Observer

> ## "*Usually when a new coach arrives, there's old-coach bashing. Okay, none of that will exist.*"
> —Tyrone Willingham at His Introductory Notre Dame Press Conference

Tyrone Willingham

university is one of the great universities in this country. But as a football coach it is one of the great opportunities in this country. So to say it is a dream come true is true."

White appreciated the class manner in which Willingham handled media questions regarding the

actions with our football team and within the structure of this university."

Following the annual Knute Rockne Dinner in Chicago on April 11, 2003, White had more praise for Willingham.

Notre Dame Athletic Director Kevin White is surrounded by the media following the press conference to announce Willingham's hiring as head coach. White not only answered questions about Willingham, but also spoke about George O'Leary's five-day reign.
Photo by Noah Amstadter/The Observer

dismissal of former Notre Dame football coach Bob Davie and the forced resignation of O'Leary.

"Usually when a new coach arrives, there's always old-coach bashing. Okay, none of that will exist," Willingham said. "I respect what Coach Davie has done and there are many great things that he's done for and with this program. What we will be about, what I will hope to bring is consistency in everything that I do—from the manner that I walk, to the manner I talk, my

"Tyrone is a professional in every sense of the word. He enjoyed immediate credibility when he walked onto our campus," White said.

"In my view, he is one of the very best coaches in the country, in any sport and at any level. I have had the opportunity to know Tyrone for 23 or 24 years. We worked at Central Michigan together way back when [1978-79]. And in recent years I had the opportunity to observe him within the Pac-10 Conference. Of course, I was at

Arizona State and he was at Stanford. This is a guy who represents all the right ideals, and he is a wonderful institutional fit at a place like Notre Dame. To me he aspires to be at the pinnacle as a coach at the elite level. And I think all of those ideals are represented at the University of Notre Dame."

White takes particular pride in the fact that Notre Dame was the only school in the fall of 2002 to qualify all six of its teams—men's and women's cross country, football, men's and women's soccer, and women's volleyball—for NCAA tournament competition (or, in the case of football, a bowl game).

A record 40 Irish athletes earned All-America honors in 2001-02. Eight student athletes were selected Academic All-Americans in 2001-02—including four who also were athletic All-Americans.

In addition to its success in football in 2002, Notre Dame claimed the 2001 national championship in women's basketball, third-place finishes in fencing in '01 and '02, national semifinal appearances in women's soccer in '00 and men's lacrosse in '01, and a College World Series berth in baseball in '02.

"It's always important to be successful at a place like Notre Dame," said White. "The bar has been set very high. That's non-negotiable. I think excellent is the mantra across the entire institution—academically and athletically. When coach Willingham was able to come in and have immediate success, it further legitimized the move in his direction. I think many of us thought it would happen. We just didn't think it would happen so quickly. Particularly those of us who have known him for a long time."

White also is proud of the fact that Willingham has managed to overcome the odds to be successful all of his life.

"He enjoys one of the great success stories in America. The Tyrone Willingham story is one of the great success stories in our country," said White. "He represents all of the right things. What you see is what you get. This is a stand-up guy with high moral fiber. If you could have a son play for anyone in this country, you would choose

Tyrone Willingham sits with his family and Notre Dame president Father Edward Malloy during Willingham's Jan. 1, 2002 introductory press conference. From left are Nathaniel Willingham, then 11; Cassidy Willingham, then 17; Kelsey Willingham, then 13; Kim Willingham, Tyrone's wife; Coach Willingam; and Father Malloy. **Photo by Michael and Susan Bennett/Lighthouse Imaging**

A Notre Dame legend and a Notre Dame legend in the making share a moment on the sideline as Willingham speaks with Father Theodore Hesburgh. *Photo by Michael and Susan Bennett/Lighthouse Imaging*

to have him play for Tyrone Willingham. To know him is to believe that."

Willingham stood 39th in the Power 100 annual listing of most powerful people in sports by *The Sporting News*—and he was the only coach at any level listed among those 100 individuals.

He was named Sportsman of the Year by *The Sporting News*, while receiving the comment, "Restored a crucial institution to power while showing up college football's minority-hiring record."

Willingham, whose team finished 10-3 in 2002 (after a 5-6 record in '01), saw his first Irish squad double the win total from the previous season. The only other times in Notre Dame football history that happened came in the following season.

White received a two-year contract extension as Notre Dame's director of athletics in December of 2002. Appointed in March 2000, White originally agreed to a five-year contract that previously was extended by five years and now extends to 2012.

"Notre Dame has a long and notable athletic history, but these past several years have set new standards for success, and Kevin deserves considerable credit for that," said Rev. Edward A. Malloy, C.S.C., the University's president. "His passion for Notre Dame, combined with his intellect and insight, have inspired our coaches and student athletes to new heights. I am delighted to acknowledge Kevin's leadership with the extension of his contract."

White, who also teaches a master's level sports business course in the University's Mendoza College of Business, is the first Notre Dame athletic director to report directly to the university's president.

White has served on numerous NCAA committees, including the NCAA Council, formerly the association's highest governing body, as well as the executive

Coach Willingham shakes hands with Kevin White after the Irish defeated the Florida State Seminoles to up their 2002 record to 8-0.
Photo by Brian Pucevich/The Observer

Top: Willingham goes over strategy with assistant coach Greg Mattison during an Aug. 20, 2002 practice. Mattison was the only holdover on the staff from the Bob Davie era. *Photo by Tim Kacmar/The Observer*

Bottom: Coach Willingham takes questions from the media after Notre Dame's season-opening win over Maryland at the Kickoff Classic. *Photo by Brian Pucevich/The Observer*

Tyrone Willingham

committee of the Division I-A Athletic Directors Association and the Bowl Championship Series. While at Arizona State he was a member of the Pacific-10 Conference's television and bowl committees.

A native of Amityville, N.Y., White earned his doctorate from Southern Illinois University and in 1985 completed postdoctoral work at Harvard University's Institute for Educational Management. He earned his master's degree in athletics administration from Central Michigan University and his bachelor's degree in business administration in 1972 from St. Joseph's College in Rensselaer, Ind., where he also competed as a sprinter in track and field. He was awarded St. Joseph's Alumni Achievement Award in 1997. In May 2001, Kevin and his wife Jane were awarded honorary degrees from St. Joseph's.

Kevin White and Willingham share a frustrating moment on the field after Notre Dame's loss to North Carolina State in the 2003 Gator Bowl.
Photo by Lisa Velte/The Observer

"When Coach Willingham was able to come in and have immediate success, it further legitimized the move in his direction."

—Kevin White, Notre Dame Athletic Director

THE PRESSURE OF THE POSITION

*Legendary Notre Dame coach **Ara Parseghian** explains the difference between coaching the Irish and other jobs—and why Willingham is as prepared as anyone to succeed*

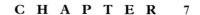

Photo by Michael and Susan Bennett/Lighthouse Imaging

Ara Parseghian is 80 years old and still lives about five miles from Notre Dame Stadium. It has been nearly three decades since he last coached the Fighting Irish. Yet for those who follow Notre Dame football, it seems like only yesterday that Parseghian guided his teams to national prominence during an 11-year span (1964-74).

"My last game was Jan. 1, 1975, in the Orange Bowl [a 13-11 win over Alabama]. My last full season was 1974," Parseghian recalled. "I watch a lot of college football on television now. Every Saturday from 11 a.m. to 11 p.m.—I really love college football. It was part of my life all of those years."

Similar to thousands of Notre Dame fans across the country, Parseghian has been revitalized by the infusion of enthusiasm created by the arrival of Tyrone Willingham to the South Bend campus.

"I had a chance to get to know Tyrone before the [2002] season started. We played a couple of rounds of golf together, so I felt I got to know him," said Parseghian. "He is a terrific guy, a very high-class guy. Watching him

during the course of the season, I thought he did a terrific job. Particularly with the difficulty of the schedule early in the season—I mean no one was predicting 10-3. People were predicting .500.

"But he got them on the road and he got them believing and got momentum going in their favor. Beating Florida State on the road? I mean, who would have figured that one out? They did a terrific job, particularly defensively. Their offense never got on track like I think they will as time moves forward and he is able to put in the kind of personnel that he would like for his attack. But they never made the mistakes that created problems for the defense until later on in the year. Mistakes made by the offense contributed to a couple of the losses. But all in all, he did a remarkable job, in my opinion."

Parseghian, who compiled a 95-17-4 record at Notre Dame, watches in astonishment the changes in the game of college football since he last coached.

"Certainly the kids are much larger. They are faster and they are better trained. And there is better equipment

"He is a terrific guy, a very high-class guy. Watching him during the course of the season, I thought he did a terrific job."
—Ara Parseghian, Notre Dame Head Coach, 1964-1974

Tyrone Willingham and Ara Parseghian, the only two Notre Dame coaches to begin their careers with an 8-0 record since Jesse Harper in 1913-14, pose together in Notre Dame's Monogram Room.
Photo by Michael and Susan Bennett/Lighthouse Imaging

Surrounded by a game-day atmosphere like none other, Willingham enters Notre Dame Stadium before the Notre Dame-Stanford game in 2002. *Photo by David Gonzales/Gonzalesphoto.com*

available compared to back in the day that I coached," he said. "I think the kids coming out of high school are better prepared and physically much larger with greater speed. From a motivational standpoint, I don't think things have changed. I think kids still go out and give it their best, and a good coach gets the best out of his team. But I think they are dealing with more talented kids today.

"I just don't think that our 1966 team, which was a national championship team, or our 1973 Notre Dame team could measure up physically to the top teams that are playing today. Almost all of them have 300-pounders all across the offensive line today. The quarterbacks are huge—six-four or six-five and 220 pounds or more. And they can move, they've got speed. The same way with the running backs. It's hard for a youngster [from the '60s] to admit we couldn't compete at that level. Some of them could, but not many of them."

Some 37 years later, Parseghian is still asked about his fourth-quarter strategy in the battle of unbeatens—Notre Dame (8-0) vs. Michigan State (9-0). The game ended in a 10-10 tie in 1966, and Parseghian was criticized for playing too conservatively at the end of the game to preserve the team's No. 1 ranking.

"It was of great agitation to me when right after the game we were being criticized, I felt, unjustly," Parseghian still maintains. "The game ended in a tie. There was nothing I could do about it. Nothing [Michigan State coach] Duffy Daugherty could do about it. I coached the team from the sideline. I called many of the plays during the course of the season. And then all of a sudden, someone else [media] was going to coach my team and say what I should do with the team.

"The bottom line of it was that we won the national championship. We had another game to go [against

Notre Dame played in the national spotlight several times in 2002. Here Willingham speaks with a sideline reporter during the Notre Dame-Air Force game, shown nationally in prime time on ESPN.
Photo by Brian Pucevich/The Observer

Southern Cal]. Michigan State did not. We were on the road in East Lansing, Mich., and I had my starting quarterback [Terry Hanratty] out of the game in the first quarter [and replaced by Coley O'Brien]. I had my starting center [George Goeddeke] out of the game in the first quarter. I had the starting left halfback [Nick

just as criticized the other way: 'What the hell are you doing? You're trying to move the ball against the wind? You're going against the No. 1 defense in the country, and you did what? You put the ball up?' Anyway, that's the way coaching is."

With the clock ticking towards an almost certain defeat, Willingham watches Arnaz Battle scurry towards the end zone to top Michigan State in East Lansing. The win ended a five-game Fighting Irish losing streak at the hands of the Spartans. *Photo by Lisa Velte/The Observer*

Eddy] out of the game in the first quarter. I had a backup halfback [Bob Gladieux and then Rocky Bleier] out of the game. I was sitting on the road in a big game with much of the talent on the sideline with me because of injuries. We were fighting the wind in the last portion of the game. It was just one of those things where everyone wanted an outcome to the game.

"If I had made some stupid mistake [in the fourth quarter], with their great kicker [Dick Kenney], they would have kicked a field goal, and I would have been

Parseghian, who followed Notre Dame coaching legends including Knute Rockne, knows what it means to be the head football coach at Notre Dame.

"I think there is pressure in coaching anywhere you go. I came from Northwestern to go to Notre Dame. I had been in the Big Ten eight years and I thought I would be able to handle all of this stuff. At Northwestern there had been [fan and media] interest within about a 500-mile radius. I didn't get calls from the North, East, West or South. But when I got to Notre Dame, all of a sudden

Willingham concentrates on the sideline during the 2002 Notre Dame-Navy game in Baltimore. The Irish had to come from behind in the fourth quarter to top the lowly Midshipmen. **Photo by Brian Pucevich/The Observer**

I realized: 'Why is this guy from Los Angeles calling me? And why is this guy from New York calling? And why is Atlanta? Or Miami? Or New Orleans? Or Dallas?'

"All of a sudden I realized that Notre Dame is a national institution. As a result, it's high-profile. So, yes, there is pressure. But much of the pressure is self-inflicted. You put a lot of pressure on yourself because you know you have to win. There are a lot of coaching jobs out there today where if you don't deliver a reasonable product, you are not going to be around very long. It's just that pure and simple.

"I think in the coaching profession, you are aware of it. You have a three-year contract or a five-year contract—that's what happened to Bob Davie. He had a couple of good years and then at the end of five years he was just barely over .500. The odds are that you are going to be replaced. That's the same case for anyone in a high-profile job. Look at professional football or baseball or basketball. You have got to deliver."

Parseghian realizes the major college coaching landscape has changed dramatically since he toiled along the sidelines.

"There is not much advice I can give Tyrone Willingham, because he is experienced," said Parseghian. "He has been an assistant coach in college football and pro football. And he has been a head coach in big-time college football. I think he understands and knows what has to be done. He recognizes that last season is history and that next year is the most important thing that is facing him. He also knows that if his record is around .500 at the end of five years, the odds of him being around are the same as anyone else's who coaches at that university. The way I see it is that he has a terrific staff, he's a great motivator and he knows what he is doing because he is experienced. I don't want to make any predictions, but my personal feeling is that he is going to be very successful at Notre Dame."

As this USC fan at the Los Angeles Coliseum boldly predicted with a T-shirt, Notre Dame's hopes of qualifying for a BCS bowl berth ended with a 44-13 defeat at the hands of the Trojans. *Photo by Brian Pucevich/The Observer*

"I don't want to make any predictions, but my personal feeling is that [Willingham] is going to be very successful at Notre Dame."

—Ara Parseghian, Former Notre Dame Head Coach

Willingham glances at his play card during Notre Dame's home win over Pittsburgh in 2002. *Photo by Cristina Reitano/The Observer*

Irish quarterback Carlyle Holiday missed most of the Gator Bowl with an arm injury. Without Holiday, the Irish struggled, ending their season with a 28-6 loss to North Carolina State. ***Photo by Lisa Velte/The Observer***

Tyrone Willingham

Right: Coach Willingham and his new team celebrate with the Kickoff Classic trophy after defeating Maryland 22-0 to open the 2002 season. *Photo by Nellie Williams/The Observer*

Bottom: At the press conference to announce his first recruiting class, Coach Willingham smiles as he answers questions. That class included Maurice Stovall and Rhema McKnight, two receivers who contributed immediately as freshmen. *Photo by Brian Pucevich/The Observer*

"I COULDN'T BELIEVE IT"

*Former Notre Dame and NFL star **Chris Zorich** explains why Willingham's hiring restored his faith in his alma mater and the hopes of the Irish football program*

Photo by Michael and Susan Bennett/Lighthouse Imaging

The impact of Tyrone Willingham being named the head football coach at Notre Dame resonates well beyond the school's campus and current players on the roster.

Chris Zorich, captain of the Fighting Irish football team his senior year, says he wishes he could have played for Willingham.

"The implications of this are huge, gigantic," says Zorich. "I mean, the fact that there are only three black coaches who are heading Division I schools...for the University of Notre Dame to make this type of decision is absolutely unheard of."

The former Notre Dame All-American defender and seven-year NFL veteran has amassed at least as many accolades off the field as on. He established the Christopher Zorich Foundation in 1993, in memory of his late mother who raised him as a single parent on Chicago's tough South Side. The Zora Zorich Scholarships are bestowed annually at Notre Dame, Indiana, and Lewis University in Romeoville, Illinois.

"She instilled in me the understanding that each person is important and special, which is how I view each client," said Zorich. In 1993 he also established Zorich Industries, Inc., a marketing and consulting firm that advises business people and high school, college and professional athletes seeking personal and financial success.

Scholarships also are issued in partnership with the Chicago Public Schools and to an institution specified each year by the United Negro College Fund—programs providing cultural, educational and entertainment opportunities to economically disadvantaged youth.

Corsages and personal care gifts are delivered on Mother's Day to women's shelters throughout the city. Thanksgiving grocery deliveries are made to hundreds of families. He is currently employed by the Chicago law firm Schuyler, Roche & Zwirner, P.C.

Zorich, who played for Lou Holtz at Notre Dame, feels that his perspective of his alma mater changed with the arrival of Willingham.

Chris Zorich celebrates a successful Notre Dame play. The All-American lineman played for the Chicago Bears and Washington Redskins in the NFL after graduating from Notre Dame in 1991. Photo by Michael and Susan Bennett/ Lighthouse Imaging

"The implications of this are huge, gigantic."

—Former Notre Dame All-American Chris Zorich on Willingham's Hiring at His Alma Mater

Former Irish All-American Chris Zorich, left, poses with Coach Willingham and former Irish defensive back D'Juan Francisco in 2002. *Photo by Michael and Susan Bennett/Lighthouse Imaging*

"I have had my own personal issues with the University of Notre Dame," said Zorich. "These are issues of not having enough students of color, things like that. Combine that with the old [Bob Davie] coaching staff. For some reason, they considered me like a plague over there. And I have no idea why.

"When I was a law student there at Notre Dame, I volunteered numerous times to do anything from going out to some of the football practices and listening to some of the guys. But as far as getting a chance to spend some time with these guys, it just never happened. I was made to feel unwelcome. It wasn't the university or the athletic department. It was the football staff. Because I was a [law] student there, I could have gone to lunch with some of the recruits, I could go to lunch with players. It was kind of free reign because I was a student there. However, I was never, ever used.

"Now, I am not trying to pat myself on the back, but if you have got a guy who played in the NFL for seven years, who started a not-for-profit foundation, who was an All-American there, won the Vince Lombardi Award, was a captain on the national championship team, and now was going to law school...I would be beating down my door if I was the head coach at Notre Dame. But my understanding was that there were some huge ego problems with Lou Holtz and Bob Davie. I think a lot of it had to do with him saying during the [assistant coach's age discrimination] trial that Holtz wasn't sane, or something like that. They had some issues back and forth. So I was considered to be one of Holtz's guys. I never ever did anything with [Davie's] team, which is just unreal."

That unwelcome feeling began to change for Zorich with the arrival of Willingham.

"I believe Notre Dame hired Coach Willingham on Jan. 1, 2002. My bank was not open on that day. So I went there the next day and went to my safety deposit box and put my national championship ring on that we had won in '88. Now, I had never worn that ring since we won it. Why? Because of a lot of issues I had with the university. Plus, on top of that, I didn't feel welcome there after Holtz left. Naming Coach Willingham meant total elation for me. During that whole coaching-search process, I was doing interviews on the radio and in newspapers. People were asking me: 'What about coach Willingham?' And I flat-out said it: 'There is no way Notre Dame is going to hire a black coach.'

"When you look at the enrollment of black students at Notre Dame, it's less than two percent. So for me, I thought hiring a black coach was just not going to happen. I remember being out to dinner with former Notre Dame quarterback Tony Rice. He is now in South Bend working for *Blue & Gold* magazine. We went out to dinner with one of his friends, and the friend was trying to convince us that Notre Dame was going to hire Coach Willingham. I was also shooting e-mails back and forth to former players that I know. And I said this is never going to happen, because we all knew Notre Dame would never, ever hire a black coach. Then Jan. 1, 2002 rolls around. I couldn't believe it."

In law school, Zorich volunteered at the Notre Dame Legal Aid Clinic, a nonprofit organization providing free legal assistance to those unable to pay.

"I was on break at the time as a law student, and when I got back I contacted Coach Willingham's office," recalled Zorich. "I sent him a letter saying 'You don't know me; I am an alum going to law school now. And I am very honored that you are now associated with the university. There are a couple hundred thousand instant Notre Dame fans because you have been named the head coach.'

"He called me a couple of days later and wanted me to come by his office so we could have a sit-down meeting. I met with him for like an hour and was just so impressed. I wish I could play for him. I walked out of that meeting very, very proud to be from the University of Notre Dame."

Always one to give back, Chris Zorich has done extensive volunteer work, including his work with Texas Children's Hospital during the holiday season. *Photo courtesy of Notre Dame Sports Information*

Top: Notre Dame students make a "W" with their fingers to show their support for their new head coach during Notre Dame's 2002 win over Pittsburgh. *Photo by Andy Kenna/The Observer*

Bottom: After a 6-0 start, Irish fans' enthusiasm for their new coach reached a peak level before the Notre Dame-Air Force game in Colorado Springs. *Photo by Nellie Williams/The Observer*

Wearing "Return to Glory" T-shirts that became the theme for the 2002 season, Coach Willingham celebrates with famous Notre Dame alumnus Regis Philbin at a pep rally. **Photo by Michael and Susan Bennett/Lighthouse Imaging**

From January to May of 2002, after I finished law school, I think I did seven or eight events with the football program as far as talking to recruits, taking them to dinner and just doing the whole thing. I felt terrible that I only had four months to actually do it in."

Zorich says he is most impressed with the fact that Willingham sees beyond the player as simply an athlete.

"I saw a television show called *Up Close* that featured Coach Willingham. It was amazing, because it didn't look like an interview of a head coach of a university; it was more like he was a CEO. You saw a president or a manager. He talked about different ways to rise to levels of success, and he just went on and on," said Zorich. "That made me think that if you had him in your living room talking to your son about coming to the University of Notre Dame, how could you not send your kid to the University of Notre Dame?"

As much as Zorich lauds Notre Dame for selecting Willingham as head football coach, he questioned the school's initial hiring of George O'Leary, the former Georgia Tech coach who admitted misrepresenting himself on his resume before resigning in disgrace.

"A lot of people said that Notre Dame gave the job to Willingham so he could fail. Then the university could say: 'See, we tried a black coach and he failed.' Then they could go out and find somebody else," said Zorich. "I was shocked at the person the university first chose, because at Notre Dame we talk about academics and athletics and we are able to have a different type of student athlete. O'Leary's graduation rate at Georgia Tech was something like 33 percent. So I was really shocked. And a lot of alumni that I talked to were really shocked.

"With Coach O'Leary, you kind of had the sense that he wasn't anybody special. If you walked into your local tavern, he would be sitting at the end of the bar. You could spend time talking to him and, you know, BS with him. But he was not that type of guy to be the head coach at the University of Notre Dame.

"Even at his Notre Dame press conference, I watched and he said he had never been there before. He talked about academics and how it was going to be a good mix between academic building and sports. You kind of got

Zorich averaged over 100 tackles a game with the Bears. When his contract with the Bears expired, he finished his pro career with the Washington Redskins in 1997. That is when he began pursuing a law degree.

Zorich is appalled at the small number of African-American head coaches in Division I football today.

"We all know that it is all about the money. And who provides money? Alumni. You have to make alumni happy.

Notre Dame fans celebrate in the stands during the Notre Dame's upset at Florida State in 2002. *Photo by Nellie Williams/The Observer*

the sense from his press conference that he was just saying the right things."

Zorich says he is more than an esteemed and highly decorated former Notre Dame football player. He is now a ticket-toting fan.

"This is the first time I have ever owned season tickets. Last year I was at every home game. For me, this is kind of a reawakening, so to speak," he said.

"Here's one of the biggest problems—athletic directories and universities are afraid. Let's not BS anybody. If you want to be a head coach at a major university, you have to be a politician. You have to be able to raise funds, you have to be able to mesh and be buddy-buddy with the alumni, mainly. And a lot of people are afraid because of their alumni. So these presidents are wondering: 'How are my alumni going to interact

> ## "This is the first time I have ever owned season tickets. Last year I was at every home game."
> —Chris Zorich, Former Notre Dame and Chicago Bears Lineman

The enthusiasm returned to the student section at Notre Dame in 2002—and these Irish fans wore it on their chest.
Photo by Nellie Williams/The Observer

The morning after the 2002 Notre Dame-USC game in Los Angeles, Coach Willingham signs an autograph for a young Irish fan at the Notre Dame Club of Orange County Eucharistic Breakfast. ***Photo by Michael and Susan Bennett/Lighthouse Imaging***

At the pep rally before the Notre Dame-Michigan game, Willingham called ESPN broadcaster Dick Vitale out of the stands to speak to the crowd. Vitale was in attendance as a fan—his two daughters attended Notre Dame. *Photo by Michael and Susan Bennett/Lighthouse Imaging*

with this black guy when they don't have anything in common?' Obviously I am making a huge generalization, but I think that is a lot of the fear that schools have."

As a fan in the stands at Notre Dame Stadium, Zorich hears and sees almost everything now.

"It was kind of interesting last season, because I attended all of the games, and when Coach Willingham didn't do something they liked, some of the fans called him 'Willie,'" said Zorich. "It kind of reminded me of the segregation era that I have read about, when black men were addressed as 'Uncle' or their first name. Never by 'Sir' or 'Mister.'

"On the other hand, the fans would make a huge 'W' in the stands for Willingham. It was an emotional experience for me. Growing up in an all-black environment and now doing the type of work that I do, seeing the sort of mecca of college football honoring a black man as a head coach...it was an emotional thing for me."

Social change has been gradual at Notre Dame, according to Zorich, but he has noticed differences since his undergraduate days.

"I have talked to some of the people in the Notre Dame admissions department. And we have the largest black enrollment ever. They are calling it the 'Ty Effect.' No one at the university will talk about that publicly. Just the thought of something like this happening—the ripples are just going to be amazing," said Zorich.

"Thank goodness for athletic director Kevin White. He was hired and then we got some black assistant athletic directors. That has never happened before. It has been frustrating, because as players you saw no people of color in administrative positions on the athletic side. Yet you can recruit us and tell us it is going to be a great experience. How does that work out? So that was a big coup when Kevin White came here. In the past, all the people who became athletic director came from Notre Dame. Now all a sudden Kevin White comes in from Arizona State and he shakes things up a little."

In an effort to get fans more involved at pep rallies, Willingham would hold out his fingers, yell "Hut!" and have the fans cheer in response. Here he holds up two fingers before the Notre Dame-Pittsburgh game. ***Photo by Michael and Susan Bennett/Lighthouse Imaging***

CHAPTER 9

RETURN TO GLORY

Dave Duerson *explains how Willingham's approach carried Notre Dame from controversy and mediocrity back into college football's elite*

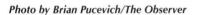

Photo by Brian Pucevich/The Observer

So what really happened behind the scenes when Notre Dame hired former Georgia Tech football coach George O'Leary, only to find out he had lied about having a master's degree?

"It was embarrassing," said Dave Duerson, a former Notre Dame captain and NFL standout. A member of the board of trustees of his alma mater, Duerson was part of a six-person selection committee to hire a successor to Bob Davie.

"Due to a selfish and thoughtless act many years ago, I have personally embarrassed Notre Dame, its alumni and fans," O'Leary said in a statement to the university. "The integrity and credibility of Notre Dame is impeccable, and with that in mind, I will resign my position as head football coach, effective December 13, 2001."

Duerson was more stunned than any of the legion of Notre Dame fans.

"When I got the call that O'Leary had stepped down, I felt like I had personally taken a shot in the gut," said

Duerson. "The reason behind that is that when we flew down to Atlanta to interview George, we went around and around after we had dispensed with all the formalities. Then I asked him one question, which was: 'Coach, what is your biggest pet peeve?' He looked me in the eye and said: 'Dave, I demand of my players and my coaches: Don't lie to me. Don't you ever lie to me.'

"So Father Malloy asked me if I had anymore questions. I said, 'Absolutely not. He is a man of integrity; that's all I am looking for.'"

Duerson felt confident after the face-to-face meeting with O'Leary that Notre Dame had found the right man.

"We had our criteria. Just in terms of the selection committee getting a feel for who that coach would be and somebody who would represent us well—we were trying to find a comfort level," said Duerson. "The one thing that was critical in my mind—as a six-man selection committee—was looking for support. But at the end of the day we were charged with hiring the most high-profile individual at our university, for 100,000 graduates and

Notre Dame's "Return to Glory" theme made its way into the stands at Florida State. And Notre Dame's resurgence continued with a resounding victory. **Photo by Brian Pucevich/The Observer**

> "[Willingham] took a program that, in essence, was about to sign off on its recruiting class. And he almost took those guys to the national championship."
>
> —Dave Duerson, Former Notre Dame Captain and NFL Standout

probably 100 million faithful around the world. So I personally felt like I had taken a shot in the gut.

"For us to get that thing rectified by getting the right guy and then being able to squelch that whole debacle as quickly as we did, I think says a lot about our program. And that we were hell-bent on finding the right guy."

Within a couple of weeks, Notre Dame hired Tyrone Willingham.

"Since I was a member of the selection committee, I am just very excited that we did a thorough process," said Duerson. "In the end, we held to everything that was our criteria. When all was said and done, the best man to fit the job was Tyrone Willingham. It was particularly gratifying for me because we got a guy of African-American descent. Yet at the end of the day, it's a shame that here we are in 2003 and race is still an issue. But that is a fact. Race matters. In one year, Ty has been able to transcend all of that. To the point that throughout the country, without exception, everyone recognizes that he is in fact a great coach. He took over a program that, in essence, was about to sign off on its recruiting class. And he almost took those guys to the national championship. He turned that program around in a matter of months."

Willingham's ambitious and expeditious plan impressed Duerson.

"Typically, you hear of coaches, and CEOs, for that matter, who generally take three to five years to get the

George O'Leary spoke to a packed Joyce Center at Notre Dame upon his hiring as Notre Dame's head coach. Within a week, he resigned as inaccuracies on his résumé were revealed. "It was embarrassing," said Dave Duerson, a member of the search committee.
Photo by Nellie Williams/The Observer

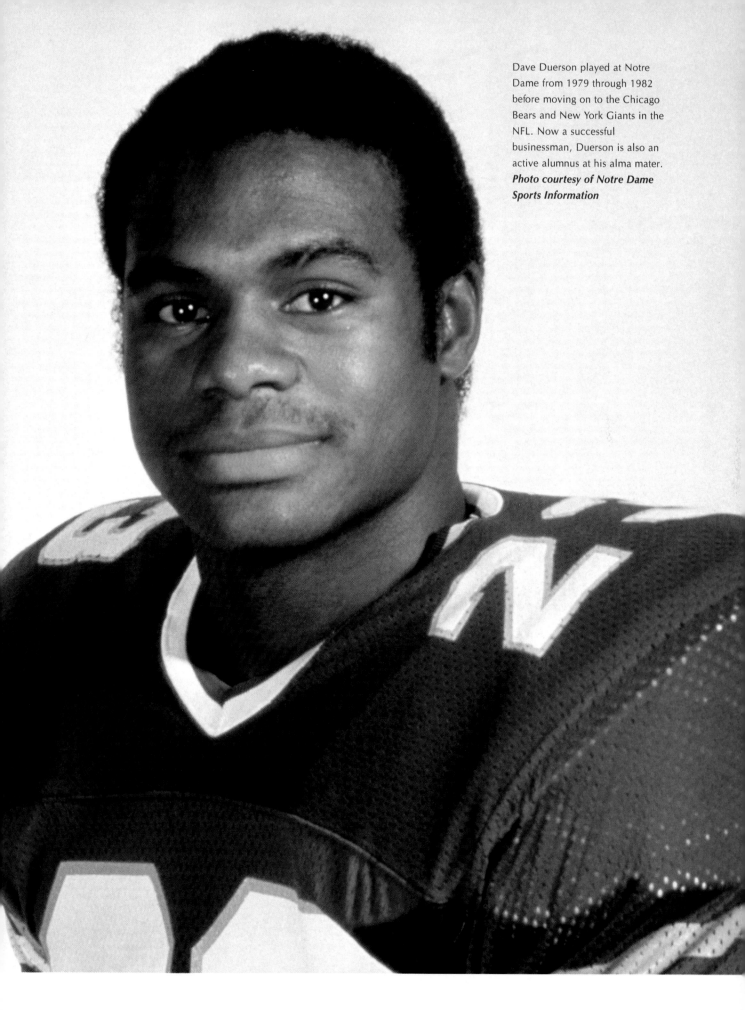

Dave Duerson played at Notre Dame from 1979 through 1982 before moving on to the Chicago Bears and New York Giants in the NFL. Now a successful businessman, Duerson is also an active alumnus at his alma mater. *Photo courtesy of Notre Dame Sports Information*

ship turned around. In very short order, Ty had all those guys running through walls for him," he said.

"Not only that, he brought the mystique back to South Bend. And that was gratifying for me as a former player and captain of Notre Dame's football program. But that is what I have heard from everybody—the mystique is back. And you see it with the number of alums and monogram winners who have come back to campus."

Duerson says he is intrigued by the possible national ramifications of Willingham being hired by Notre Dame.

"I'm watching. In fact, I'm keeping score," said Duerson. "Without question, this should open additional doors. There should be no question in anyone's mind that African-Americans are qualified to coach Division I football programs. Not just at black colleges, but at major colleges across this country. When you look out there and 65 to 70 percent of the athletes playing Division I college football are African-American, and an even greater proportion of those are the impact players on your football

While the Irish struggled on offense during Willingham's first season at Notre Dame, defense and special teams often saved the day. Here safety Gerome Sapp carries a fumble recovery in for a touchdown against Purdue. *Photo by Andy Kenna/The Observer*

Tyrone Willingham

With its strong alumni base and support amongst American Catholics in general, Notre Dame football has a throng of fans everywhere it goes. Here a couple of young fans in Baltimore cheer on the Irish against the Midshipmen of Navy. **Photo by Brian Pucevich/The Observer**

team, it's criminal. It really is. It's criminal that there are only three or four black head coaches at the Division I level and three in the National Football League."

If a historically conservative school such as Notre Dame can change with the times, why can't other renowned universities?

"You just look at our recruiting at Notre Dame in this one year," said Duerson. "There are parts of the country, particularly in the South, where we can go get that big nasty defensive lineman that we couldn't have gotten in the past. Or that aggressive offensive lineman. Every coach in the country, particularly in the Southeast, used the fact that Notre Dame was a Catholic institution and predominantly white with about a three percent African-American population. They used that against us

in recruiting. That, they can no longer say. All of a sudden, we are attractive to the rest of the country.

"One of the other gratifying things to see has been the number of African-Americans who quickly became Notre Dame fans. That was good to see. For me, being a former player and captain and most valuable player and now a trustee—to see BET [Black Entertainment Network] and different shows with people in the audience with Notre Dame shirts on is amazing. Both black and white people. It was just exciting. It lets you know without question that the Notre Dame brand is strong. And it is great to see Notre Dame back in the forefront where it should be."

Duerson is president/CEO of Duerson Foods. After graduating from Notre Dame, he played for eleven

Irish fifth-year senior receiver Arnaz Battle eludes a Pittsburgh defender. Battle, a quarterback his first three seasons at Notre Dame, was one of Notre Dame's veteran leaders in 2002. *Photo by Andy Kenna/The Observer*

Tyrone Willingham

seasons as a safety in the NFL and was a member of two Super Bowl championship teams (1985 Chicago Bears and 1990 New York Giants).

In 1994, Duerson began a new career as a McDonald's franchisee. He was approached by their corporate headquarters to become a primary breakfast sausage supplier to their system. Duerson relinquished his franchise and purchased the majority interest in Fair Oaks Farms, L.L.C. in 1995. In February, 2002, Duerson sold his majority interest in Fair Oaks Farms. He then took his executive team along with him and established Duerson Foods, L.L.C.

The pride and networking opportunities afforded Notre Dame alums has not been lost on Duerson. There is an old joke that if you get 1,000 guys in a room, how do you know which one is from Notre Dame? "Because he will tell you," said Duerson with a laugh. "That's probably pretty true.

"Our university has changed a great deal in the last three or four years. For instance, I have become the first African-American president of the Notre Dame Monogram Club. I have been going through this process of second vice president to first vice president. So this becomes a first. And then behind me is a female that I selected. We're trying to open this thing up. It has been a conservative university, without question. Up until the early '70s, Notre Dame was all male. So a lot of change has taken place.

"In fact, in the last couple of years, we have actually had more female students on campus than male. The university has undergone great change. And I think Tyrone becoming our head coach is at the epicenter of it and the climax of change. Particularly since Notre Dame is viewed as the premier college football program with all the tradition that goes along with it. For him to be at the helm just says a great deal about where our program is headed. And we like being proponents for change. Hopefully, the rest of the country will grab hold of that and give African-Americans and other minorities who have great football minds and coaching ability the

Despite their overwhelming early success, media observers continued to doubt the Irish. Here, ESPN's Lee Corso predicts a Florida State victory over Notre Dame in Tallahassee. *Photo by Nellie Williams/The Observer*

opportunities to become coaches if they are in fact the best qualified ones for the job."

Duerson is confident that Willingham will continue to emphasize foremost the importance of a Notre Dame education.

"Everything I have ever been involved in, both business and philanthropic, Notre Dame was in the mix," said Duerson. "Whether it was banking relationships or the six years that I was with WGN Radio when I was with the Chicago Bears. The Tribune Company's board said they wanted to do a radio show with the Bears during the time we were gearing up for Super Bowls. They said: 'Well, there is only one man for the job—Dave Duerson.' That's because the bulk of the board at the Tribune Company at that time were Notre Dame alums."

Tyrone Willingham

"[Willingham] brought the mystique back to South Bend. And that was gratifying for me as a former player and captain."
—Dave Duerson, 1982 Notre Dame Captain

Notre Dame's defense embarrassed well-respected offenses all season long in 2002. Here the defenders celebrate a turnover against Florida State. **Photo by Nellie Williams/The Observer**

Cornerback Shane Walton, who came to Notre Dame in 1998 as a soccer player, capitalizes on a Maryland turnover in the 2002 season opener. *Photo by Brian Pucevich/The Observer*

Tyrone Willingham

But Duerson realizes there are many doors that still remain difficult to crack open, even for someone who is as qualified as he is.

"Being in business now, even with the success we have had with my former company Fair Oaks and now Duerson Foods—we still have to fight the 'dumb jock' syndrome," he said. "It's always going to be tough for athletes in business because of the stereotype. And that is particularly true when you are a black athlete. But Notre Dame squelches a lot of that. And it helps that I went to Harvard and went through their program. The bottom line is a quality education and a branded university speaks volumes in the business world. That was the key. That's why I chose to go to Notre Dame as an 18-year-old kid out of Muncie, Ind."

With Notre Dame returning to the forefront of prominent football powers in the nation, Duerson sees the program having the same appeal that it did when he was a youngster.

"From the time I was in seventh grade, all four foot, 10 inches, 83 pounds of me, I wanted to go to Notre Dame," he said. "I had just watched the movie *Brian's Song*, and that is what inspired me to want to play full-contact football. And that same year I was writing a book report on Rocky Bleier, writing about his experience in Vietnam and having taken some bomb fragments. He heard people say he would never walk again. His response was: 'Not only am I going to walk again, but I am going to play in the National Football League.'

"That inspired me. Also, Luther Bradley was from the same junior high and the same high school I attended and he had gone on to Notre Dame. So I told my parents I was going to play at Notre Dame. My dad put his hand on top of my head and said: 'Son, just keep your grades up and we will do what we can.' Everyone thought I was going to end up being a runt."

A third-round draft pick of the Bears, Duerson was one of three 1983 draftees who started and became a significant member of defensive coordinator Buddy Ryan's record-breaking unit. Seven starters on that Bears Super Bowl XX championship team were acquired in the 1983 NFL draft, making it possibly the best draft by any team ever.

Pushups in the stands, a tradition in the student section at Notre Dame, are seen in Tallahassee during Notre Dame's win over Florida State. *Photo by Nellie Williams/The Observer*

"My dad worked at General Motors for 38 years. It was a proud moment for both my mom and dad when I went to Notre Dame. We still talk about it almost every time we get together. Mom is 81 and Dad is 80. With all of my success in the NFL and the things I have going on in business now, my Dad just says: 'You never know what a rusty-kneed kid is going to grow up to be.'"

Notre Dame students storm the field after the Irish upset Michigan early in the season. Asked after the game what he thought of the scene, Willingham responded, "Help." ***Photo by Nellie Williams/The Observer***

"PROUDER THAN I WAS ON THE DAY THAT I GRADUATED"

*Chicago Bears assistant and Notre Dame alum **Greg Blache** expects Willingham's dynamic personality and approach to have far-reaching effects*

Photo by Tim Kacmar/The Observer

reg Blache was one of just a handful of African-American student athletes on the Notre Dame campus when he began his college career in the late 1960s.

Coaching became an integral part of his life in 1968 when he became a defensive assistant at Notre Dame. As a freshman, Blache had suffered a leg injury that ended his playing aspirations. Upon graduation in 1971, Blache remained at Notre Dame for five seasons, one year as a graduate assistant and four years as a full-time assistant.

Blache later joined the Tulane staff in 1976, where he coached the offensive line (1976-77), outside linebackers (1978-79) and defensive backs (1980). He returned to Notre Dame to coach running backs (1981) and the defensive line and outside linebackers (1982-83). He served one year as defensive coordinator with the USFL's Jacksonville Bulls in 1984 and had one-year experiences at Southern University (1986, defensive coordinator) and Kansas ('87, special teams coordinator) before going to Green Bay in 1988.

A defensive back at Notre Dame before his injury, Blache earned a bachelor's degree in sociology and a master's in secondary education.

Prior to joining the Bears, Blache served as the Indianapolis Colts' defensive line coach for five seasons (1994-98) and held the same position for the Green Bay Packers for six years (1988-93), where he served on the staff with Dick Jauron. At Indianapolis, Blache was an assistant under Ted Marchibroda, Lindy Infante and Jim Mora and helped the Colts advance to the AFC title game in 1996. He coached several top pass rushers at Indianapolis, including double-digit sackers Dan Footman and Tony Bennett along with tackle Ellis Johnson.

His success as a defensive coach has earned Blache NFL head coaching considerations both after the 1998 and 2001 seasons.

Now the highly regarded defensive coordinator of the Chicago Bears, Blache considers it a matter of

> # "By far, [Willingham] was the most qualified individual Notre Dame could have hired."
>
> —Greg Blache, Notre Dame Graduate and Former Assistant Coach

Willingham eyes the field during the Notre Dame-Boston College game in October, 2002. The loss marked Notre Dame's first defeat under Willingham. *Photo by Lisa Velte/The Observer*

Greg Blache came to Notre Dame in the late 1960s as a defensive back, but a leg injury ended his playing days and sent him into the coaching ranks. He served as an assistant at Notre Dame under Ara Parseghian, Dan Devine and Gerry Faust. ***Photo Courtesy of Notre Dame Sports Information***

After a loss to Boston College and a lackluster effort against Navy, the Fighting Irish got back on track with a 48-0 trouncing of Rutgers in the final 2002 home game. Here, Arnaz Battle races to the end zone. **Photo by Andy Kenna/The Observer**

personal pride that his alma mater hired Tyrone Willingham as its head football coach.

"By far, he was the most qualified individual Notre Dame could have hired. If they wanted someone from a good academic institution [Stanford] who had success on the collegiate level—this guy had it," said Blache. "I know they bounced and bandied other names around, but I am just glad that when it came time to pull the trigger, athletic director Kevin White had the courage to recognize that this guy was best for the university. And I think it speaks volumes for Kevin as a leader and a guy

in management. And it speaks volumes for the University of Notre Dame to back him on it.

"Other institutions across America recruit African-American athletes, but they are scared to death to pull the trigger when it comes to putting those guys in the seat to run those programs. By Notre Dame doing that, I was proud of that day. Prouder than I was on the day that I graduated."

Blache remains hopeful that the long-range ramifications of Willingham's hiring will impact many other colleges across the nation.

"It was huge, and I was glad that Notre Dame was one of the first of the big schools to do it," he said. "With the small number of African-American head football coaches in America, it is almost to the point where it becomes laughable. Years and years ago in the '70s when I came in, people said there were not many of us qualified. Quite honestly, in this day and age, they can't use that excuse anymore. There are a lot of older guys like myself who have no interest in going back to the collegiate ranks to go through all the headaches and hassles you have to go through. But at the same time there is a huge group of very talented, well-trained, honest and clean-living black men going through the collegiate ranks right now. I see [white] coaches being fired for this and fired for that. All kinds of off-the-field issues. And yet the schools continue to just work that pool. It comes to the point where you say: 'What is it going to take?' I hope we are turning the corner and I hope we are starting to move forward. But only time will tell."

Blache and Willingham have monitored each other's careers both on and off the field.

"I have known Tyrone ever since he was at Michigan State. A long, long time," said Blache, a 15-year NFL coaching veteran. "Then he went to the Minnesota Vikings [as an assistant coach]. He is one of the brightest, classiest people both in and out of football. He has got a lot of charisma, a lot of presence. And he is very knowledgeable in the game of football.

"He is a good recruiter and he has done a phenomenal job at Notre Dame. When he got the job I

Known to bring out the best in his players, here Willingham congratulates Irish quarterback Carlyle Holiday during Notre Dame's win over Rutgers. *Photo by Andy Kenna/The Observer*

Tyrone Willingham

was really excited. He is the best hire they have had since Ara Parseghian. And I mean that sincerely. This guy belongs at Notre Dame."

Blache has the football background and credentials to know what it takes to be successful in the college and professional ranks.

In 2001, Blache shaped the Bears into one of the top defensive units in the NFL, producing the top-ranked scoring defense in the league. That Bears unit allowed only 203 points in 16 games (12.7 points per game), which ranks third in Bears history for a 16-game schedule behind only the 1985 and 1986 Bears. In his first three seasons, his defense accounted for 11 touchdowns (two in 1999, four in 2000, five in 2001).

Chicago's 2001 defense, led by All-Pro first-team members Mike Brown, Brian Urlacher and Ted Washington, ranked second in the NFL and first in the NFC in rushing yards allowed per game, allowing 82.1 yards per contest. The 2001 Bears only surrendered three rushes of over 20 yards all season and six rushing touchdowns, the fewest since 1998 (five).

Now Blache sees the selection of Willingham at Notre Dame as a portent of great seasons ahead for the Fighting Irish.

"The head coach is sort of like a hood ornament. He is the first thing you see," said Blache. "He is a great hood ornament because of the way he handles himself and presents himself and the way he can communicate with people. I think he is a very special person, but he would be successful in anything he chose to do. If he wanted to go into business and be the CEO of a company, he could do that. If he wanted to be a great high school or elementary school teacher—the guy has got ability and people skills that a lot of the rest of us just wished we had. Once you meet him, you never forget him, because he is such a dynamic personality. Not a pushy personality, but he shows you he is genuine and

The Irish cornerback tandem of Vontez Duff (standing) and Shane Walton shut down some of the top receivers in America during the 2002 season. *Photo by Nellie Williams/The Observer*

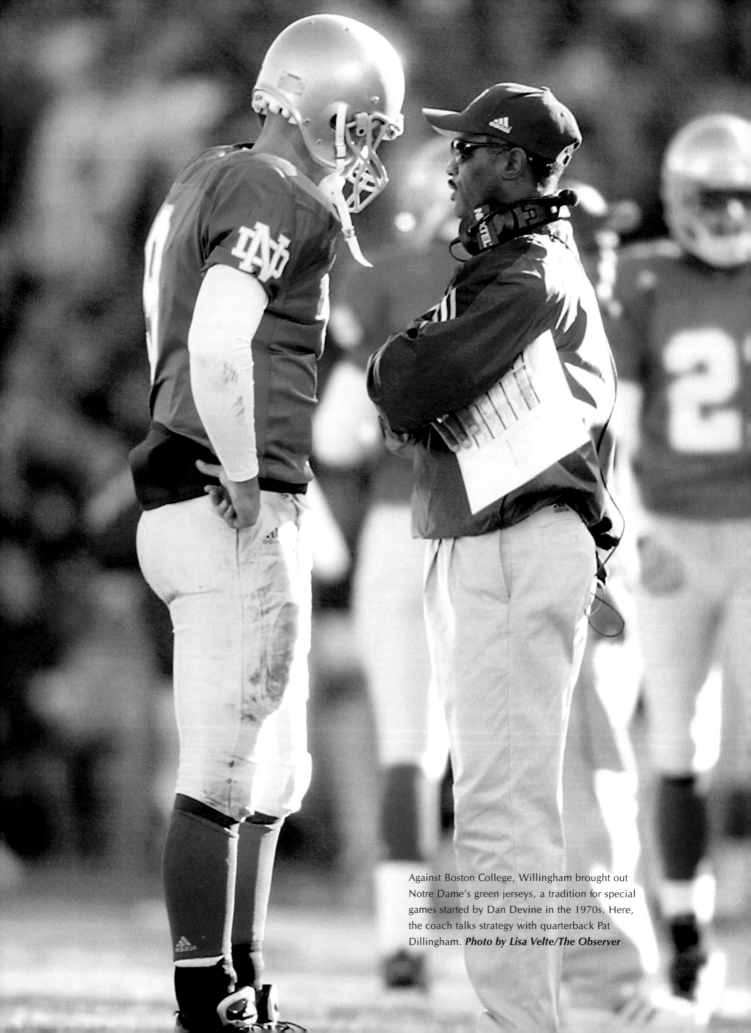

Against Boston College, Willingham brought out Notre Dame's green jerseys, a tradition for special games started by Dan Devine in the 1970s. Here, the coach talks strategy with quarterback Pat Dillingham. *Photo by Lisa Velte/The Observer*

Before the Notre Dame-Air Force game in Colorado Springs, Willingham poses with MSgt. Todd Tureskis, left, and SSgt. Brian Gilliland.
Photo by Michael and Susan Bennett/Lighthouse Imaging

"[Willingham] can walk into the home of anybody in the United States and sell the university. I think it is a perfect match."

—Greg Blache, Chicago Bears Defensive Coordinator

Gracious in victory as well as defeat, Willingham shakes hands with Pittsburgh wide receiver Chris Curd after the Irish defeated the Panthers.
Photo by Tim Kacmar/The Observer

sincere. All of my friends back in South Bend found that out right away. And that's why the players like to play hard for him. He took a team of guys that weren't expected to be that good. Even in the NFL draft, how many of those guys got drafted?

"Jeff Faine is the only guy who got drafted halfway early. But Notre Dame beat a lot of good football teams. So there is a lot of excitement back in South Bend again because they have a guy similar to Parseghian with the class and ability to recruit. He can walk into the home of anybody in the United States and sell the university. I think it is a perfect match."

Blache acknowledges that becoming the head football coach at Notre Dame requires unique qualities.

"Notre Dame is not for everybody. Everybody cannot fit at Notre Dame, because of the academic demands, because of other demands. But this guy is a perfect fit for Notre Dame," he said.

"With certain schools, when you read the newspaper and they are always coming up with different problems," said Blache. "Not that Notre Dame has been totally clean the last few years, but it is nothing like some of these schools that have renegades and rogues there. Notre Dame has a lot of sharp young men who are students first and athletes second."

It has been over three decades since Blache walked the Notre Dame campus as a student. Blache, 54, is married (Lynn) and has six children: Greg, Jr., Jennifer, Christopher, Sarah, Corinne and Matthew. My, how the times have changed.

"When I went to Notre Dame, there were eight black students on campus. There were 19 in my freshman class. We took the total up to 27," Blache recalled. "Larry Schumacher was a sophomore linebacker, and Ernie Jackson and I were the only three on the football team. There were two blacks on the basketball team.

"It was unique. Coming from the South [New Orleans], I had never gone to school with white kids before. I had been educated during segregation. So it was very competitive, but it was a unique experience at Notre Dame. Being from the South, the diet was different,

Willingham's intensity and frustration increase as time winds down in Notre Dame's loss to Boston College. ***Photo by Lisa Velte/The Observer***

Willingham instructs his Fighting Irish players during Notre Dame's loss to USC. *Photo by Nellie Williams/The Observer*

the sense of humor was different, everything was different. It was like I had been dropped on another planet almost. But we had each other. The black basketball players and I were very close. Bob Whitmore took us under his wing, and he was sort of our mentor on campus. He showed us the ropes.

"I walk that campus nowadays, and I can't believe it has come this far in the period of time. When I was there, Notre Dame was an all-boys school. You had to sign in the dorms every night. You had to sign out if you wanted to leave campus over the weekend. We had lights out at 11 p.m. We had to wear shirt and tie for dinner and all meals on Sunday. We were on honor code, and it was strict. But I wouldn't trade it for anything. The experience prepared me for what I do right now. It prepared me to deal with another culture on a daily basis. It prepared me academically; it prepared me to take what my parents had given me and polish it more and take it further. I was fortunate to come across some phenomenal people at Notre Dame. There isn't a time when people ask me about Notre Dame that I can say anything but rave things. I can't say the weather was good, because it wasn't. Or that the food was good, because it wasn't. But the people were good and the experiences were good. And there were people who bent over backwards to make sure we all succeeded. From the day you walked into the school and until today, there is a network of people I can go to if I ever need them."

Notre Dame walk-on running back Tim
O'Neill raises his helmet in celebration
after Notre Dame's victory over Stanford.
Photo by Cristina Reitano/The Observer

Against Rutgers, the final home game for each of their careers, Arnaz Battle (left) and Shane Walton thank the fans for their support.
Photo by Chip Marks/The Observer

"Notre Dame has a lot of sharp young men who are students first and athletes second."

—Greg Blache, Notre Dame Classes of 1971 and 1973

Tyrone Willingham

In his first season as head coach, Willingham's ability to get the most out of his players resulted in taking the same group of athletes that finished 5-6 under Bob Davie to an 8-0 opening mark and a 10-3 finish. *Photo by Michael and Susan Bennett/Lighthouse Imaging*

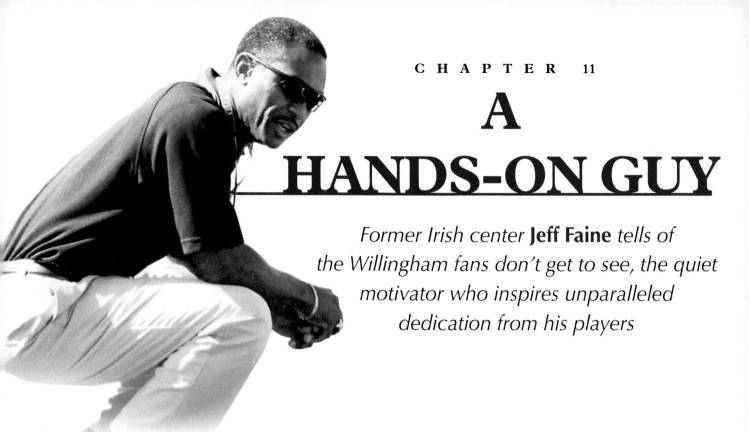

A HANDS-ON GUY

*Former Irish center **Jeff Faine** tells of the Willingham fans don't get to see, the quiet motivator who inspires unparalleled dedication from his players*

Photo by Michael and Susan Bennett/Lighthouse Imaging

Jeff Faine was bracing for another tumultuous season on and off the field with the Notre Dame football team in 2002. Coach Bob Davie had been fired, and his immediate successor, George O'Leary, was forced to resign soon after accepting the job.

Then came Tyrone Willingham.

"I had a pretty good relationship with Coach Davie," said Faine, the star center for the Fighting Irish who was a first-round draft pick of the Cleveland Browns in April, 2003.

Faine redshirted as a freshman and then went on to start every game for the next three years at center, becoming a first-team All-American in 2002.

"At first it was tough because I was recruited by Coach Davie and I played for him for three years. I had really grown to like him a lot. But as I gave Coach Willingham his chances, or just kind of opened up to him, he turned out to be just an unbelievable coach and an unbelievable man and an unbelievable leader. To be able to come in and do what he did...to the public, I don't think most people understand exactly what he has done, just to be able to take a team that had played under another coach and to get the whole team to buy into what he was teaching and his philosophy in the first week that he was there.

"That whole last three years at Notre Dame saw Coach Davie's job being discussed constantly—whether he was going to get fired or not. Then there was Coach O'Leary coming in and that whole ordeal. But in the end I think Notre Dame came out on top. They got a very promising coach and promising future for Notre Dame."

The future also looks bright for Faine. The six-foot, three-inch, 303-pounder was a finalist for the Rimington Award, which goes to the nation's top center. He won Notre Dame's Nick Pietrosante Award as the player who best exemplifies courage, loyalty, teamwork, dedication and pride. Faine did not allow a sack as the Irish averaged 313.5 yards per game his senior year.

Coach Willingham surveys his new team at an April 23, 2002 practice. *Photo by Nellie Williams/The Observer*

Former Notre Dame center Jeff Faine, drafted in the first round of the 2003 NFL draft by the Cleveland Browns, walks off the field after the 2003 Gator Bowl, his final collegiate game. **Photo by Lisa Velte/The Observer**

"The Browns want me to be at the weight I am now, whatever I can be productive at," said Faine. "I feel comfortable at this weight."

Faine was so big as a child that he wasn't permitted to play youth football.

"It was real frustrating," he said. "I'd run in the street with trash bags on my body trying to get my weight down, but I just couldn't. I was like 50 pounds over."

After starring in high school in Sanford, Fla., Faine was recruited by all the national powerhouse schools: Notre Dame, Miami, Florida, Florida State and Ohio State. His second choice was Miami, where Browns coach Butch Davis was then head coach.

All four of the schools, except for Notre Dame, played for the national championship during his college years.

"But I never regretted it," Faine said. "I felt great about my decision and I still do."

As the 21st overall pick in the NFL draft, Faine knows the spotlight will be on him.

"I don't want to let these guys down for taking a gamble and picking me in the first round," he said. "I want to come out here and really provide them with what they thought I had."

Controlling his weight might be easier than controlling Faine's emotions in practice and in games.

"Probably the most difficult thing for me was trying to control Jeff in practice," Irish offensive coordinator

"As I gave Coach Willingham his chances…he turned out to be just an unbelievable coach and an unbelievable man and an unbelievable leader."
—Jeff Faine, 2002 First-Team All-America Center

Bill Diedrick told the *Cleveland Plain Dealer* after the Browns selected Faine in the draft.

"He was the most intense young man I've ever been around."

Faine received two personal fouls in the Gator Bowl and had several shoving matches with E. J. Henderson against Maryland last year.

"You know those shoving matches you'd see him in on game day?" Diedrick said. "He was the exact same way on every drill and in every scrimmage. It wasn't an intent to hurt, just an intent to prove 'I'm bigger, more physical, faster.'

"He was guilty for most of the penalties," Diedrick said. "Probably a couple were cheap, but I'm sure most were well-deserved. We were constantly trying to educate him on the difference between finishing a play and going too far. But he grew in that area and learned how to tone it down so that it didn't hurt the team."

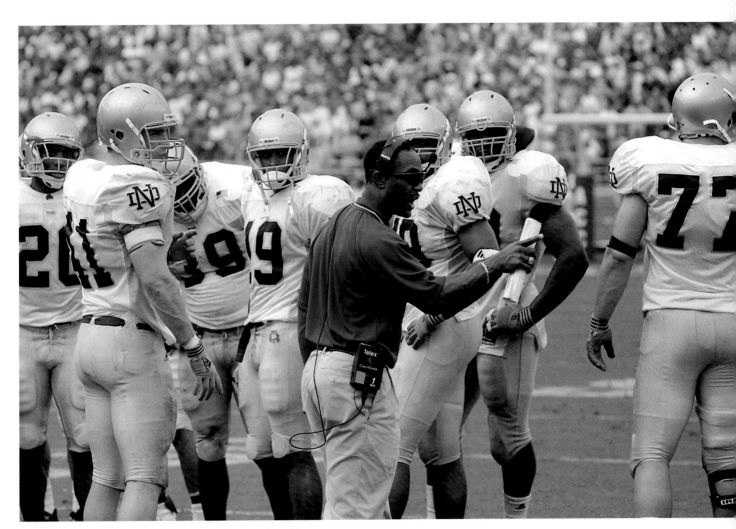

Coach Willingham instructs his troops on the sideline during Notre Dame's 2002 win over Florida State. **Photo by Brian Pucevich/The Observer**

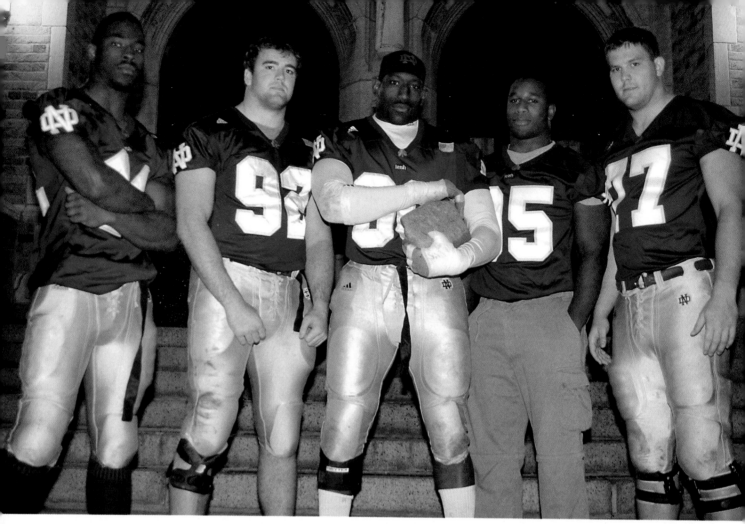

While the defensive backs got the majority of the publicity, Notre Dame's defensive line was the "rock" that held the defense together in 2002. Shown from left are Justin Tuck, Kyle Budinscak, Darrell Campbell, Ryan Roberts and Greg Pauly. *Photo by Nellie Williams/The Observer*

Faine is renowned for being a punishing blocker who was able to pancake-block many of his opponents in college.

Diedrick and Faine's position coach, John McDonell, said Faine also was regarded the emotional leader of the Notre Dame team.

"He set the tone and made the others around him that much better," Diedrick said. "The defensive coaches were always mad at me for how hard he went in practice," McDonell said. "But I loved it."

Faine registered 102 key blocks/knockdowns while grading 84 percent for blocking consistency. He was clocked at 5.27 seconds in the 40-yard dash, and he bench-pressed 365 pounds.

But Notre Dame was unable to win consistently during Faine's career until Willingham took over.

"The whole Coach O'Leary thing left a dark spot on Notre Dame's history," said Faine. "But it turned out to be one of the brightest spots that has ever happened. To have an opportunity for Coach Willingham to come in after that whole foul-up, I mean, that might have been the best thing to happen to Notre Dame. I think he has got the program headed in the right direction."

Faine said his legendary shoving matches during Notre Dame practices were not calculated.

"For me, I wasn't trying to disrupt his practices or anything. But I did have to tailor myself to be able to fit in his program," he said. "At some practices I had to hold back on some things that I used to do. I knew I couldn't do those things anymore. And really it was for the good of the team. He has a certain schedule for things to get done and he is trying to fit enough plays in. A wasted rep is something you can't get back in practice. We worked together and we got things ironed out. Things went smoothly."

Despite the uncertainty surrounding the Notre Dame head coaching situation the past few years, Faine said he and his teammates never seriously considered transferring.

"Not that I ever heard," he said. "It was exciting for Coach Willingham to come in. All of those good things we had heard about him were only half true. The truth is tenfold as far what really goes on with Coach Willingham and his program."

Faine was the only Notre Dame player selected in the first round (21st overall) of the 2003 NFL draft, which says a lot about the job Willingham and his staff did to lead the Irish to a 10-victory season.

"I think there is some kind of dark cloud over Notre Dame," said Faine of the dearth of top draft picks.

"Hopefully, with me being able to sneak up in [the first round], maybe we can break that. There is some quality talent at Notre Dame, and now they have someone there to point that quality talent in the right direction. I think Coach Willingham is definitely doing that. Within the next few years, I think there will be more Notre Dame players taken in the first round. He will be able to recruit, because people want to play for Coach Willingham. As

Coach Willingham leads his seniors onto the field before the 2002 Michigan game. Behind Willingham are, from left, Jeff Faine, Gerome Sapp, Shane Walton and Glen Earl. *Photo by Cristina Reitano/The Observer*

On the sideline at Air Force, Willingham looks out onto the field. *Photo by Michael and Susan Bennett/Lighthouse Imaging*

With a whistle around his neck, Willingham inspects his troops at the team's last practice before the season opener against Maryland.
Photo by Brian Pucevich/The Observer

time goes on I think the talent pool will get better. They will get more of the blue-chippers and more of the high-profile running backs."

The transition to the NFL will not be easy for Faine. But his Cleveland Browns teammates liked what they saw of him in minicamp following the draft.

Starting right tackle Ryan Tucker talked to Faine about making the adjustment to the NFL.

"I wanted to come in and see what kind of a guy he is," Tucker told reporters. "He's articulate. He's not a meathead like a lot of us. I have confidence that he can learn stuff and make calls. I think he'll be a great addition to this team."

Tucker noted that two prominent former first-round linemen, Orlando Pace of the Rams and Damien Woody of the Patriots, "got torched" in their rookie seasons.

"It's hard, man," said Tucker. "This is my seventh year, and in all that time, I've seen maybe five offensive linemen plug right in and excel right away."

But there's no substitute for experience.

"Some guys figure it out quick, and some guys, it takes three years, like it did for me," Tucker said.

"I'm still trying to figure it out. It will help having some guys in there that have played a lot."

Television viewers of Notre Dame football games see a stoic-looking Willingham on the sideline. He measures his words during halftime and postgame media interviews. But what is Willingham like with his players behind closed doors?

"Behind closed doors, he opens up a little more," said Faine. "There is nothing like his pregame talks. Just as a picture is worth a thousand words, I think one of

Irish All-America center Jeff Faine
releases the ball to backup quarterback
Pat Dillingham against Stanford.
Dillingham, who attended high school
in California with Tyrone Willingham's
daughter, led the Irish to victory.
Photo by Lisa Velte/The Observer

Coach Willingham's words is worth 100 words. He really doesn't have to say much to get the point across. He picks his words so well. But I have never been more prepared or more pumped up to play a game than when he would get us ready. He would just find a certain way to do it. He walks around the locker room, almost like he is trying to pick a fight. Not challenging anybody, but he is just walking around, talking to everybody on the team from the starting quarterback to the walk-on free safety. He talks to everybody because his philosophy is: 'Who knows who is going have to make a play that day?' Everybody is prepared to play when the football is kicked off."

While many college football head coaches rely on their assistants to convey a message to their players, Willingham generally takes a more direct approach.

"Coach Willingham is a hands-on guy," said Faine. "He is not really dependent on his assistant coaches to communicate his messages. He wants them to communicate their own messages. When he has something to say, it is definitely getting said."

What began as an uncertain 2002 senior season for Faine turned out to be an exhilarating ride of a lifetime.

"This has been a learning experience, and I have learned tons from it. I am sure it can do nothing but help me in the NFL," said Faine.

"It is still pretty hard for me to take it in that I am not a part of the Notre Dame team any more."

At a pep rally before the Notre Dame-Boston College game, Coach Willingham reacts to a humorous speaker.
Photo by Michael and Susan Bennett/Lighthouse Imaging

At one of the first full-squad practices in the fall of 2002, Willingham puts the Irish through a running drill. *Photo by Brian Pucevich/The Observer*

"I have never been more prepared or more pumped up to play a game than when he would get us ready."

—Jeff Faine, Irish Senior in 2002

Never one to stand by idly while making others work, Willingham encourages players and participates in workouts, as he did at this Aug. 28, 2002 practice. ***Photos by Brian Pucevich/The Observer***

CHAPTER 12

A PROMISING FUTURE

As Willingham's first recruiting class begins to contribute, the future appears bright for Fighting Irish football

Photo by Michael and Susan Bennett/Lighthouse Imaging

Tyrone Willingham set the bar high in 2002 for an encore performance. Ever the perfectionist, Willingham looked at the challenging 2003 Notre Dame schedule with visions of even greater success.

The annual Blue-Gold intrasquad game on April 26 at Notre Dame Stadium finished off a successful spring practice session. The scrimmage offered an opportunity for reserve quarterback Chris Olsen to excel. He was involved in 23 of the 31 points scored by both units.

But it was the Irish defense that continued to shine in the Blue-Gold contest after propelling the team in Willingham's initial season.

The Blue team forced three second-half turnovers, all leading to points, in a 17-14 victory over the Gold. Olsen played for the Gold in the first half and Blue in the second.

"I thought he did a good job," Willingham told reporters later. "I was impressed with how clever he could be at times. He made some plays; that is always a good quality for a quarterback."

Olsen was 11 of 25 passing for 146 yards and ran for a four-yard touchdown.

Offensive coordinator Bill Diedrick said he was impressed with the sophomore, who did not play in a game as a freshman.

"He stepped up and made some plays," Diedrick said. "He showed maybe a little more consistency than he has."

Olsen ran the scout team last fall.

"Just because it was the rest of the scout team, the rest of the freshmen, running against possibly the best defense in America," Olsen said. "It helped me a lot."

Olsen expressed hope to be given the opportunity to challenge Carlyle Holiday for the starter's job. Pat Dillingham was the backup quarterback in 2002.

"Time will tell," Willingham said.

Dillingham helped Notre Dame to wins over Michigan State and Stanford in 2002. He completed five of twelve passes with two interceptions in the Blue-Gold game.

Irish quarterback Carlyle Holiday releases a pass over the Rutgers defense en route to a 48-0 victory in 2002. Holiday enters the 2003 season as the incumbent starter at quarterback with two years of eligibility remaining. *Photo by Chip Marks/The Observer*

Holiday played only two series because Willingham wanted to get a better look at Olsen and Dillingham.

The Blue offense was limited to minus-13 yards total offense in the first half. In the second half, the Blue defense forced three turnovers. Jake Carney intercepted a pass by Dillingham that bounced off Maurice Stovall and returned it 24 yards to set up a 27-yard field goal by Nicholas Setta.

Defensive end Travis Leitko later recovered a Dillingham fumble at the Gold 26-yard line.

The Blue offense picked up its first first down with 6:35 left in the third quarter when Olsen threw an 11-yard pass to Omar Jenkins. Olsen then threw a 21-yard pass to Jenkins on the two-yard line to set up a TD run by Jeff Jenkins on the next play.

Two plays later, Jared Clark bobbled a pass from Dillingham that Vontez Duff intercepted at the Gold 48-yard line. A 28-yard pass from Olsen to Jenkins helped set up Olsen's four-yard TD run, giving the Blue a 17-6 lead.

The Gold managed a 74-yard scoring drive, including a 39-yard pass from Dillingham to tight end Anthony Fasano, to cut the lead to 17-12. The Gold added a two-point conversion when Dillingham tossed a pass to Clark in the back of the end zone. Right guard Sean Milligan is the only returning starting lineman for the Irish.

"We've still got a lot of work to do," Willingham said. "We're still learning. We're still growing. That's a big area of concern."

*"We've still got a lot of work to do.
We're still learning. We're still growing."*
—Tyrone Willingham on the Notre Dame Offensive Line

Coach Willingham talks with Irish kicker Nicholas Setta before the 2002 season opener against Maryland. Setta, one of the most prolific kickers in Notre Dame history, enters his final season of eligibility in 2003. *Photo by Michael and Susan Bennett/Lighthouse Imaging*

While some key members of the 2002 Irish defense graduated, two keys to the unit's success return as seniors in 2003—cornerback Vontez Duff, shown above scoring against Maryland, and linebacker Courtney Watson, seen below gaining yardage against USC.
Photos by Brian Pucevich/The Observer

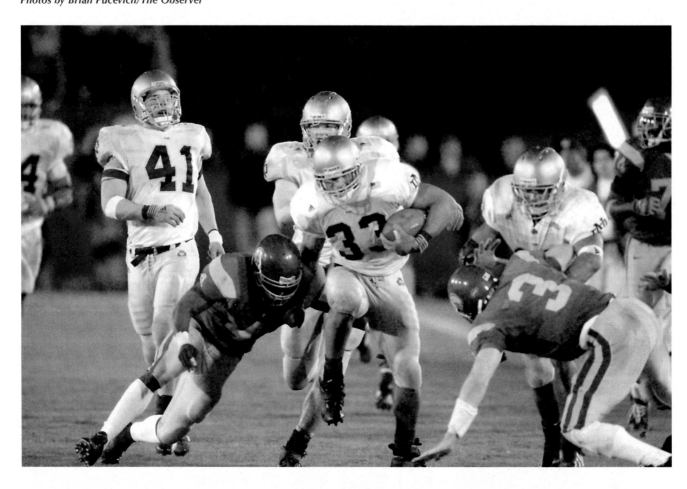

Tyrone Willingham

Originally recruited as an option quarterback by Bob Davie and Kevin Rogers, Carlyle Holiday has had to adjust to Willingham's "West Coast" offense. Here, Holiday gets to run against Purdue.

Photo by Andy Kenna/The Observer

With the departure of starting offensive lineman Jordan Black, Jeff Faine, Sean Mahan, and Brennan Curtin for the NFL, Notre Dame's biggest adjustment in 2003 will be a revamped offensive line. Here the new line gets to block for quarterback Chris Olson (12) and running back Rashon Powers-Neal (32) in the 2003 Blue-Gold Scrimmage. *Photo by Michael and Susan Bennett/Lighthouse Imaging*

Quarterback Chris Olson, who never saw the field as a freshman, was 11 of 25 passing for 146 yards in Notre Dame's annual Blue-Gold Scrimmage in April, 2003. *Photo by Michael and Susan Bennett/Lighthouse Imaging*

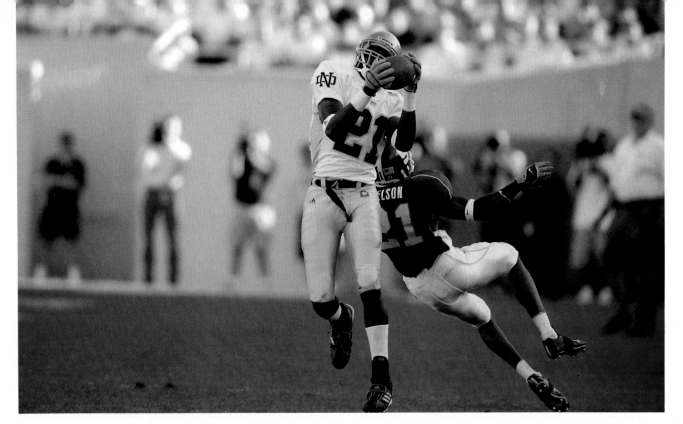

Top: One of Willingham's first recruits, freshman receiver Maurice Stovall made multiple key receptions in 2003, including this one against Michigan State. *Photo by Lisa Velte/The Observer*

Bottom: After Irish quarterback Carlyle Holiday left the Gator Bowl with an injury, the Irish offense was rendered ineffective against North Carolina State. The Irish look to have much greater depth and experience at the quarterback position in coming seasons. *Photo by Lisa Velte/The Observer*

Given the bulk of the snaps at quarterback in the April, 2003 Blue-Gold Scrimmage, Chris Olsen was involved in 23 of the 31 points scored by both units, and impressed head coach Tyrone Willingham with his cleverness.
Photo by Carrie Peters/The Observer

Celebrate the Heroes of College and Pro Football
in These Other 2003 Releases from Sports Publishing

George Toma:
Nitty Gritty Dirt Man
by Alan Goforth

• 6 x 9 hardcover
• 250 pages
• color photos section
• $22.95

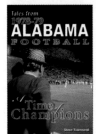

Tales from the
Sooner Sidelines
by Jay Upchurch

• 5.5 x 8.25 hardcover
• 200+ pages
• photos throughout
• $19.95

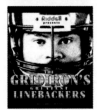

Tales from 1978-79
Alabama Football:
A Time of Champions
by Steve Townsend

• 5.5 x 8.25 hardcover
• 200+ pages
• 20-25 photos throughout
• $19.95

Riddell Presents:
The Gridiron's
Greatest Linebackers
by Jonathan Rand

• 8.5 x 11 hardcover • 160 pages
• 50+ photos throughout • $22.95

The Fighting Irish
Football Encyclopedia:
Third Edition
by Michael R. Steele

• 8.5 x 11 hardcover • 530 pages
• 200+ photos throughout • $39.95

Otis Taylor:
The Need to Win
by Otis Taylor
with Mark Stallard

• 6 x 9 hardcover
• 250 pages
• eight-page photo section
• $22.95

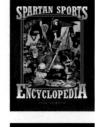

The Spartan Sports
Encyclopedia
by Jack Seibold

• 8.5 x 11 hardcover
• 700+ pages
• photos throughout • color foldout
• $49.95

Tales of the Iowa
Hawkeyes
by Ron Maly

• 5.5 x 8.25 hardcover
• 200 pages
• 25 photos throughout
• $19.95

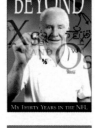

Beyond Xs and Os: My
Thirty Years in the NFL
by Jim Hanifan with Rob Rains

• 6 x 9 hardcover
• 250 pages
• eight-page photo section
• $22.95

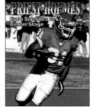

Tales from Penn State
Football
by Ken Rappoport

• 5.5 x 8.25 hardcover
• 200 pages
• 25 photos/drawings throughout
• $19.95

Priest Holmes:
From Sidelines to
Center Stage
by Bill Althaus

• 8.5 x 11 hardcover
• 250 pages
• color photos throughout
• $24.95

Marcus Allen:
The Road to Canton
by Marcus Allen and Matt Fulks

• 8.5 x 11 hardcover
• 128 pages
• color and b/w photos throughout
• $24.95

To order at any time, please call toll-free **877-424-BOOK (2665)**.
For fast service and quick delivery, order on-line at **www.SportsPublishingLLC.com**.